Embodying Reality

Embodying Reality

A new paradigm for sustainability

Casper Stubbé

ANIMI
PARTNERS

©2022 Casper Stubbé

First edition: november 2022
Publisher: Animi Partners
Editor: Nahual Lhorente
Design: Haags Bureau | Boekenmakers
Print: IngramSpark

www.embodyingreality.com

ISBN 978-90-831859-3-4 (print)
ISBN 978-94-644371-9-5 (e-book)
NUR: 400

All rights reserved. No part of this book may be used or reproduced in any manner whatsoever without written permission except in the case of brief quotations embodied in critical articles and reviews.

*From a life for love
to a life from love.*

Contents

Preface 9

Part 1 Trusting systems 13
There is no solution
A myth
Systems of trust
Colonizing myths

Part II Trusting life 75
Backwards
Miracle of life
Our state of being
Into the unknown

Part III Falling into reality 141
Guiding without steering
A field of energy
Healing comes to you
A sense of the sacred
Living from wisdom
A mystery
The path of the black sheep

Afterword 210
Bibliography 211

Preface

We have arrived. Most of what was predicted when I was little is now a reality. A disrupted climate, mass immigration, ecosystems in decline and an unfathomable inequality in our societies. These are examples of global crises. Crises that affect all of humanity and to which we have not found an appropriate response.

We live in a world full of people. This has never happened before and therefore it's no surprise that our current ways of thinking no longer work. Even more frightening, though, is the fact that no one has any idea anymore of what is going to happen. Since Limits to growth (1972) was first published, we know we're on a path of destruction and, so far, we have not managed to steer clear of it. Despite all the well-intended actions to do better.

This book is not an analysis of what a realistic response to global crises might be. I've done and seen enough system analysis and I don't believe we need more of them. More analysis is not going to bring the acceleration sustainability require. Embodying Reality is about a search for a new perspective from which a realistic response can emerge. A new paradigm for sustainability.

While writing, I have stayed as true as possible to my teachers and examples, which can also be found in this text. They have shown me how to enable new paradigms.

The content of this book needs time to grow into. Understanding is only the first step. What the impact of a myth is, what the experience of a wild path is, how the natural processes work and where to find wayfinders are topics you grow into slowly. It's content that continues to unfold, even if you have understood it for years. It also helps not to try to understand it using concepts you already know. As a human species, we are entering a new age and old understanding is more of a hindrance than a helpful guide when wanting to reconnect with reality as it is now.

It will also help to read this book with others. In meaningful conversations with others, the new becomes normal again and the normal becomes new again. Embodying Reality is primarily a call to start a conversation with each other about what is important in our lives and how to prioritize this in our daily life, despite social pressure and other expectations from society.

Getting a master's in sustainability and working in the field has made me believe that what is happening in sustainability will not bring a sustainable and equitable world. This is what inspired me to write this book. After writing it, I realized the things I write about are already happening all over the world. A new paradigm for sustainability is already being built and people are living it, trying it, doing it. It's just not called sustainability most of the time. I needed to learn where to look for it. I hope this book will enable you to see it happening too and inspire you to do your part wholeheartedly.

This book is for people who, as I, feel like the world is not going in the right direction and don't know if what they're doing is enough. People who are angry at the world, or who have slided into apathy. Or people who feel powerful, but don't know how to translate their energy to anything meaningful for the world. People who genuinely want to contribute to a better world, this book is for you.

The best way to read it starts with understanding that the message of this book is not in the text, but in your experience while reading it. The white space of these pages says a lot more than what the black letters can tell.

*"You, walker, there are no roads,
only wind trails on the sea."*
Antonio Machado, poet

Part 1
Trusting systems

The first thing I can remember waking up from a coma is a beige ceiling, dimmed lights, an analog clock on the wall and two pictures next to it. One of myself and one of my family. The only thing I knew for sure was that I was dying and I wanted to say goodbye to my family. The clock read three o'clock, so where were they?

My reasoning was logical, but wasn't real. A week earlier, just before the coma, I had been on the verge of death, but when I woke up, my life was no longer in danger. Also, it was three o'clock in the morning and my family was just sleeping.

During that night, I occasionally regained consciousness, hallucinating about aliens and flying beds. This continued until it was eight o'clock when my family walked in and found, to their own surprise, a cheerful Casper in his IC bed. Everything was familiar again.

I was fifteen when I went on a holiday to France with my cousin and his family. On July 14th, which is a national holiday in France, I was riding a bicycle when a drunk biker crashed into me head-on. As he was wearing a helmet, he won the head-butt. With a double jaw fracture, a crushed nasal cavity and three fractures in my eye socket, I lay bleeding on the ground. I don't remember any of this, as I don't remember pretty much anything of the 48 hours before the accident.

There happened to be a trauma doctor in the neighborhood who arrived there at the same time as the ambulance. He sent me to the best hospital and prevented me from choking on my own blood in the ambulance. Because of his skill and help, I am still alive today. There was fluid in my brain which created life-threatening pressure in my skull. Once I arrived at the hospital, they immediately induced me into a coma so that my brain would shrink and therefore reduce the pressure.

The doctors first told my parents that I probably wasn't going to make it. They got on the plane thinking they were going to collect the dead body of their son. A day later, they were saying that the coma was probably going to last six months. Two days later, the danger on my life had disappeared and, after five days, I was allowed to wake up again. Apparently, I wasn't done here, on this planet, and had beaten all the odds to get back as soon as possible. After twelve days, I was allowed to go home again.

At home, I could still do very little and spent nine weeks lying on my bed in a dark room, completely dependent on the care of others. During the first six weeks, I could only eat baby food intended for six-month old infants. I had to slurp it behind my teeth, because my jaws were clamped together with iron wires fixed to my teeth so they could heal. During the following three weeks, I either ate baby food intended for twelve-month old children, or blended food because I still couldn't chew yet. The whole process was like being born a second time. After two months of receiving the sweet care from those around me, I was able to go back to school and participate in normal life again.

If it's a gift that you are still alive, normal life doesn't seem normal anymore. Even though there's nothing notably different for me than for everyone else. We all have experienced the miracle of birth, but we don't often see it that way anymore. We live as if our birth and our death does not exist, and that is a great loss. We take life for granted, however every second of it is a miracle. Our mortality makes our existence so special and worthy of deep gratitude and wonder.

I've had an intense near-death experience and that can be very healthy. Now that I've been born twice, I can put it into words: life is the meaning of life. I still have a fear of death, but my respect for death has become greater. Ignoring death is no longer possible.

Now I have a less established plan for the future and not such a strong idea of what life is supposed to be like. Another way of saying this is that I have a more open identity. Which is quite useful when living in a human world in the middle of a transformation process. It's easier for me to let go of old stories that have worked in the past

> but no longer serve reality. All our stories and ideas about how things should be. And this change is something I'd wish for everyone.
>
> Respecting death brings you closer to reality, and that makes room for more life and freedom. It feels like seeing things from a new perspective. Everything is the same and yet everything is different.

There is no solution

Facing global crises is not very different from facing death for the first time. It's life hitting you in the head with a brick, but if you let it, it can set you on a path to a better life. If there is anything global crises can teach us, it's learning how to deal with death. Learning to accept that things cease to exist and take on a new form. We have become so afraid of death that we don't accept the fact that there are problems we have no solutions for. That's why most of us still choose to ignore the current situations of global crisis. Even though they are right in our faces. If there is no crises, there is no need for a solution.

Global crises are now a reality and no longer a scary prediction for the future. Ignoring or denying them takes us further away from reality and makes us more dependent on the plans we have for the future. It means you focus on your own life, ignoring the bigger reality you also happen to be a part of.

Unfortunately, those who are working on a solution for sustainability are not very different. Often, they are also fighting against the end of the world as we know it. Making people and themselves more dependent on their own ideas about what life should be like. Instead of reconnecting with reality first. Nowhere have I seen more ego than on sustainability events. They are so sure of their own story and good doing.

The truth is, there is no solution to the interconnected global crises of our time. It is not possible to solve the climate crisis, declining biodiversity, inequality, racism, mass extinction and ecosystem decay simultaneously and on a realistic timescale. Everything is going to change, including our perspective of what a 'solution' entails. It takes courage to step into the unknown. Which is not something you do, it is a realization. The realization is: nobody knows what is going to happen next, you're already there.

We currently perceive something as a solution only if we can maintain our way of living in the world. The acceleration we desperately need for sustainability will come when we expand our idea of what life should be like. Now we live as if reality is secondary and our ideas about life are primary. Which, of course, is the other way around.

What has brought us here is being too concerned with people's stories and plans and not paying attention to our environment enough. We have put people outside of nature and lost sight of how life works on the planet. By making new plans and stories about how we're going to solve these global crises we are unintentionally inserting the problem in our so-called 'solutions'. Namely, living with an idea of how the world should be. That's not working toward a solution, that's the problem.

The challenge before us, then, is not to come up with better solutions, but to learn how to reconnect with reality. The very paradigm from which we are currently devising our solutions is where the problem lies.

It's not about preventing global crises. It's not about learning to deal with global crises either. It's starting from the awareness that we are the crises.

For example: calling the climate crisis the "climate crisis" is misleading. There is nothing wrong with the climate, it's working quite well and even responding somewhat predictably to human activities. The crisis is that we humans are no longer listening to the environment and are putting our own ideas about life as the most important issue. We prioritize our ideas of life and even exploit reality in order to develop them. Of course, that's the wrong way around.

The struggle that exists is not with the world, but with ourselves. The climate crisis is in ourselves, not in the climate.

Respecting death is one of the most important and most difficult parts of this process. If we connect with reality again, then we will also encounter death and the cruelty of nature. Working on sustainability should start with this. Guiding people in reconnecting with reality and remembering to see the difference between the things that are real and the things we make real.

A good metaphor for attaining a new paradigm is that of walking through a door, or a gate, into a new space. What our response to global crises requires is for us to find the courage to let go of what is familiar and walk through the gate into an unknown space. Any story you give to this unknown space brings you right back to the space where you started. Making life more complicated instead of more real.

This is a completely different option than the two alternatives the UN gives us for a path towards sustainability. The UN is working on mitigation and adaptation. Mitigation means to try to prevent future problems and adaptation means to adapt to current problems. What else is there? Well, both still assume humans and their ideas as the center of existence. This assumption is what has to change.

The UN could be the institution that makes nations part of a whole again, instead of enabling the parts to exploit the whole more peacefully as it's unintentionally doing now. The UN keeps nations at the center of power but, of course, the planet is the center of power. There is no healthy nation without a healthy planet. A better name for an institution fighting for the whole would be the United People and not the United Nations.

What the philosophy of mitigation and adaptation lacks is room for a new paradigm. If we really want to ignite massive collective action, it's not going to be like something we've ever seen or done before. Including what we have been doing for sustainability until now. Pushing solutions for parts of the crises is distracting us from working on our paradigm, our dominant ideas about life. It promotes the illusion that we know what is going to happen. We don't.

The approximately 500 million indigenous people in the world have been saying and living this forever. Sustainability in the modern world is a eighty-year-old discussion. In those discussions two perspectives can be discerned. Two stories that people rely on as a path to a solution. One story is called The Wizard, and the other story is called The Prophet. Charles C. Mann describes these stories in his book *The Wizard and the Prophet* (2018).

In the 1940s, there were two scientists who both saw the decay of ecosystems due to the growing pressure humans put on it. Both wanted to do something about it, but they had completely different reactions to it. One response has been symbolized as the Wizards, the other one as the Prophets.

Wizards rely on the narrative that with the right technology and the right policies, humans can handle all the problems in the world. They have the belief that there are not too many people on the planet, but too many people with too few tools and knowledge to handle their problems. The Wizards follow the ideas of Norman Borlaug, a scientist who used pesticide and seed enrichment to save humanity from famine.

In the 1940s and 1950s, food production could not keep up with the growing world population. Borlaug made sure that this gap was filled with smart technology and appropriate policies so that the world's population could continue to grow. He was so persistent and ultimately successful that he received a Nobel Prize for his work.

Wizards represent the power of innovation and the creative human spirit. They favor small government, because the opposite would only delay things with regulations and taxes. A free market is good, because it encourages people to take risks and develop their ideas. Money and freedom are therefore the guiding values for Wizards. This includes the belief that people are above nature and can turn it into whatever they want with their free spirit.

The story of the Prophets is based on the reaction of William Vogt. He saw the ecological decay in the world and concluded that human presence was putting enormous pressure on nature and that people should leave nature alone more often. He believes population decline is vital and it needs a strong government. A government with a strong education, informed citizens and growing prosperity must ensure that fewer children are born.

For Prophets, money is the symbol of the problem, the greed of Man who turns natural resources into money, creating mountains of waste, toxic mines and dead soil. They believe we need a strong government to counter this. Money is bad and so are people, until they leave nature alone. Veganism, community living and vegetable gardens are part of the Prophets' story, which often includes the belief that people are the problem.

Even though the Prophets' story fits better with the planet's limits and the complexity of global crises, the story hardly sells. Partly because typical Prophet solutions such as food forests, sea freighting with sailing ships and schools with vegetable gardens, among others, perish when you start applying them on a global scale. They are inspiring examples that things can be done differently, but global crises require more than inspiration alone.

The Wizard solutions have not worked either. The global crises are too complex to solve within the current systems through technology and policies alone. With finite energy, materials and time, you cannot address all global crises on a realistic timescale. Technology and policies remain stuck in the sphere of partial solutions, where they may be an improvement within a system, but cause other problems in other systems. We must start working from the whole again.

Both the story of the Magicians and the story of the Prophets were logical solutions at the time. But eighty years later, both stories no longer fit today's world. Even though most governments, corporations and rich people still follow the Wizards' story of "It's still possible!", and more and more people follow the Prophets' story of "Save us!". Both are necessary, but far from enough. Also, they keep humans and their ideas about how life should be as the central issue and look for (sustainable) ways to manipulate the outside world to make this possible. Again, this is the very cause of our problems, and shouldn't be part of the solutions.

While writing this book, I read all the Brothers Grimm's fairy tales to try to find one that could guide the message of this book. I did not find one. The current situation is unique and stories from the past are inspiring, but can't help us now. What I did find out is that the fairy tales we know are all from the seventh edition of the book. I had accidentally bought the first edition of a German to English translation.

In the first edition, the introduction states that the Brothers Grimm, two brothers from Germany, asked their intellectual network in Europe to send them the stories that were told at the dinner table at home. Therefore, they did not call their stories fairy tales, but folk tales. They also did not write the stories themselves but collected them. The original stories are much older than 1812, the year the first edition came out.

It's a romantic, idealistic and culturally significant mission. To collect the folk tales that are told to children from all over Europe. Sharing them across the continent will increase the cultural understanding between countries and unlock the wisdom hidden in them to a broader audience.

In the introduction of both the first and seventh editions, the Brothers Grimm explain this intention. Only upon reading the first story you find out both editions are not the same. The first edition didn't sell well, so the German brothers made a few changes. Six times in all, until the seventh edition finally became internationally famous and a commercial success.

For example, the stories that spoke negatively about the church were taken out so the volume could be sold through the church as well. Stories that spoke poorly of mothers were taken out or rewritten as stepmothers. The poor stepmother who left Hansel and Gretel for dead in the woods was their mother in the first edition. Also, Cinderella's horrible stepmother was her mother in the first edition.

Poor loving stepmothers and poor children of terrible mothers!

Furthermore, the stories have been adapted for the parents' convenience. Such as the adaptations they did on the first folk tale "The Princess and the Frog." It goes something like this.

A princess is playing with her favorite golden ball, until it accidentally rolls into a pond and sinks to the bottom. At the edge of the pond, she encounters a frog who is willing to retrieve the ball for her if she promises to become friends with him. She quickly promises to do so and the frog retrieves her golden ball. Overjoyed with her golden ball, she runs back to the palace. As you can imagine, the princess has already forgotten her promise to the frog.

The frog angrily comes to seek amends from the king. The king hears the frog's case and commands the princess to be friends with him. A deal is a deal.

Up to here, the first and seventh editions are the same. What happens next in the seventh edition, the one that became world-famous, is that the princess and the frog eventually become friends in her room. Until ultimately, the princess kisses the frog and the frog turns into a handsome prince. They get married and they live happily ever after.

In the first edition, the princess has no desire at all to become friends with the dirty frog. Once in her room, she deviantly throws the frog against the wall. This turns the frog into a handsome prince. They marry and they live happily ever after.

You can see how a small change in events makes the story convey a significantly different message. How would you like to raise your daughter? With a story about standing up for your own opinion or with a story about obedience? With a story of kissing a friendly frog or smashing an innocent animal to death? Exactly. As you can imagine, the seventh edition with stories about the pious church, perfect mothers and obedient daughters sold like hotcakes.

Of course, due to their huge impact, they managed to

mix the stories told throughout Europe, but they left out part of the wisdom of why they were passed on for so many generations in the first place.

In the end, the difference between the first and seventh editions portrays the message of this book. We prioritize the wrong things in our lives and the result is we are destroying the very reality we live in. We adapt our stories for our own convenience, to hide society's atrocities and ease our conscience, instead of facing reality for what it is.

The challenge with sustainability is that the cause of the problem is our current dominant idea about life. So to add sustainable ideas to our current paradigm is as realistic as the 7th edition of the Brothers Grimm's 'original' folk tales.

A myth

There is a big gap between what we know about global crises and how we respond to them. Global crises hasn't really penetrated our hearts yet. It's so much easier to just pretend the situation isn't that bad, or that someone else will solve it, or we honestly care about it but still keep doing what we've always done, or the strangest one of all, thinking it's something for the younger generation to solve.

Clearly, there is a force that is stronger than common sense. The same force that changed the Brothers Grimm's 'original' folk tales. We hardly talk about this force, because we want to believe we know reality and what we do is normal and the right thing to do. When it comes to our own lives, we have the greatest difficulty admitting that we have a limited perspective on reality. Even though we always have a limited perspective on reality. It's just part of being human.

We haven't talked about this for so long we are losing a vocabulary for it. The words I know for this unconscious force that is stronger than common sense are myth, paradigm and ego. They're different words that describe the same force in our lives.

In an intellectual context, we call it a paradigm, which is our worldview, our way of thinking. Etymologically, the word paradigm originated from: 'what stands next to it'. Our interpretation of the world therefore can be seen as a filter over reality, and we call it our paradigm. It's how we give meaning to what happens to us. Our paradigm is the source of what we think is normal, as well as the foundation of our culture.

In a spiritual context, we call it our ego. Our ego is the story we tell ourselves about who we are and what life should be about. It's our model of the world, which we defend at all costs. The effect of our ego is fragmentation and separation. Ego makes us believe that the air we breathe is ours, but the tree over there is not. Our ego is how we judge what happens to us as a success or failure. The ego makes us believe our perspective on reality is the only reality and what we do is logical, no matter what it is we do.

Myth is the word we use in the context of anthropology, philosophy and poetry. It reinforces the idea that our perspective on reality is not real, but an illusion. It's not meant as a myth like an old story about mythical gods, but our own unconscious story about life itself. We use the word myth if we want to describe the implicit story that governs our life. Or as the American Heritage Dictionary puts it: "A myth is a popular belief or story that has become associated with a person, institution, or occurrence, especially one considered to illustrate a cultural ideal." A myth dictates our perspective on reality.

You see, they are nearly the same. Our myth, paradigm and ego. Different words for the same unconscious dynamic that is stronger than our common sense and basic knowledge about reality. Something that separates us from reality and, simultaneously, convinces us it is reality.

What the Brothers Grimm eventually did to their collected folk tales is due to their myth, paradigm and ego. They wanted to sell a lot of books and they thought it was logical to adapt the stories in order to make this happen. Even if it meant lying and making people believe they were the original stories.

The same goes for the buyers of their book. If the message of the stories didn't reinforce their existing myth, paradigm and ego they wouldn't have been interested in buying it. Even though the original stories have qualities that made families tell them to their children for generations. We prefer to pretend we already know what life is about and don't buy things that don't affirm our existing idea about life. I'm no different, you're no different. This is the reality of being human. Especially when you're part of 'the modern world'.

As we grow up, we collect interpretations of what we see around us and what we experience ourselves. What we see and what we experience is reality, how we interpret them and how we name them, that's our imagined reality.

We humans walk in two worlds.
One is reality where everything is real by itself.
The other is our imagined reality.
Where everything is made real.

Reality is the world of water, air, earth, as well as our body and talents. It exists independent of our trust.

Our imagined reality is the world of countries, money, politics and our social media. It exists and has value because we put trust in them. Our myth, paradigm or ego, dictates our imagined reality. They are formed by our past and what we see in other people, especially our beloved ones.

Intense experiences have a particularly strong impact on our myth. Intense experiences, both positive and negative, form the foundations of how we view the world. A loving parent, a shameful moment at school, or a broken heart become a sort of programming we function by in the world, and we start to see the world based on our programming.

We make up a story with whatever happens to us and this forms our myth. In return, it starts to dictate how we interpret things. We become what we repeatedly do. For example, a feeling is already something, even before you give it a name. Your feeling is real, what you name it and what you do with it, that's what you make real.

"A myth is like an ecosystem. It is more than the sum of its parts, and no single event stands without the relatedness of all other parts of the story. It exists on all levels at once, material, spiritual, ecological, personal, and physical. The myth, when spoken or enacted, has meaning and potency only in the present. It takes shape according to who is telling it, what is being told, who is hearing it, and the environment or season in which the performance takes place. No matter how carefully it is studied, analyzed, and understood, the very nature of myth undoes any fixed meaning or analysis. The myth is alive – more close to truth than fact – and must be approached like wilderness, on its own terms, to be experienced fully."

Christine Downing in The Long Journey Home (1994)

The reason we don't react realistically to global crises is because of this unconscious force that is stronger than our common sense and basic knowledge of the world. Most of us ignore this force and just hope for technology or legislation to save us, so we keep adding stuff to an inherently broken system and story. The acceleration we desperately need will come when we stop adding things to an incorrect system and start reconnecting with what is real.

The challenge with this is that our imagined reality overwrites reality surprisingly easily. Our myth reshapes our idea of what is important and what deserves our attention. It makes us believe our imagined reality is reality and deserves our highest priority. So we don't see reality for what it is, we just see our imagined reality in the world. It's a self-confirming loophole and it imprisons us all.

*"We don't see things as they are,
we see them as we are."*

<small>Anaïs Nin, poet</small>

Trust is the key to the realm of myth, paradigm or ego. What we trust we call normal. And our definition of "normal" is made up of the interpretations of what we see in others. We trust what we see in others pretty quickly, and trust what we hear, or read in a book, very slowly.

People mirror themselves through life, as can be seen with children. Children rarely follow exactly what parents tell them to do, but accurately imitate their parents' behavior. So if you want to influence your children, focus on your own being. What you say to them is not that important.

People handle the two worlds very differently depending on their background. By applying strong generalizations, I can make three distinctions: Palace people, City people and Wild people.

Palace people live their lives according to the dominant story of society. They don't know any other story and if there is any other, it is secondary. They are usually theoretical educated and are only satisfied if their lives live up to their expectations. Which is almost never. They think they create all the qualities of the modern world and expect you to join their story, which is 'good for all'.

Some are very arrogant and openly affirm to do it for their own self-interest, others are even worse and claim they can help you become a part of the dominant story and be successful 'like them'. Palace people live in only one world and have an answer for everything and are dead sure about every single one of their answers. Being completely unaware there is a reality outside their imagined reality, their main concern is with their ego. However, they think it's the whole. Where they believe the whole is constructed from the parts up.

They view City people as people who just haven't understood this yet and should be either helped or exploited. They view Wild people as barbaric and reckless, people who should be tamed.

Although they rarely actually do anything in the real world, they get all the credit for what's happening in society. They do this by controlling the dominant narrative of what is normal. Usually they are restless and in a constant state of doing things. They believe children are doing good when they perform well at school, think the economy is doing well when we say the economy is growing, associate being rich with having a lot of money, think that getting married is the same as love, and that you mature by having children. They experience their myth as reality and honestly believe everybody in the world (secretly) desires their idea of success.

City people are usually trapped in the same dominant story of society, but through scarcity. They are not given a fair chance because both the story and their social context are often holding them down from climbing the social ladder (and becoming Palace people). They usually have a practical education and therefore have a better connection with reality than Palace people. They are less distracted by their myth, paradigm and ego. Also, by knowing the hardships of reality, they usually are more aware of the two worlds than Palace people. City people are often good at 'seeing through' the intentions of Palace people, but don't know how to get out of their situation due to the scarcity they live in.

City people are kept mortally afraid of the wild thanks to the dominant story and, therefore, keep trying to hold on to what is familiar. They know the two worlds, but hold on to their imagined reality out of necessity. They think it's better to live broke than to die, or worse, be shamed.

They are the backbone of the dominant story, their hands make it all possible, but they don't get the credit. They are mostly concerned with the well-being of their direct group and rarely pay attention to the whole. Having leisure time and lots of friends is their idea of being rich. They experience the myth as a prison which they cannot escape from.

Wild people choose to live outside of the dominant myth and are easily recognized by their state of being. They are not trapped by the illusions of having to constantly do something all the time, and are more present. They are open to anyone as long as they don't have to conform to their story and are allowed to live their own way. They live close to what is natural and spontaneous, and take care of the whole. They do not believe the whole is constructed from the parts up, but see the parts as a result of the whole. They prioritize the whole over the parts.

Wild people do not enjoy the comforts of the larger group and experience the hardships of reality firsthand. They live a humble life and accept it as it comes. For them, wealth is having plenty of time in nature, solitude, intimacy and playfulness. In secret, there is often much interaction between Palace people and Wild people. Where Palace people try to stay smart and sharp in their own ego systems and wild people feel validated and valuable by helping Palace people. Whereas Wild people and City people easily become friends. They both experience the dominant myth as an illusion and cannot believe that anybody could fall for its evident absurdities.

All three have their role to play and their own process of healing and contributing to the transformation the world is in. And anyway, most people are a mix of the three.

As the world is transforming in something new, both in reality and in our imagined reality, we need to let go of our own ideas about what is important. If we were right we wouldn't be in this mess. Letting go of the past completely and start living in the moment. Working on paradigms is something else entirely then working on technology, legislation, or education.

"One always lives according to a myth, for a continuous interpretation of consensus reality is inherent to the human condition. The question is whether one's chosen myth resonates with one's deepest intuitions or runs counter to them."

Bernardo Kastrup, More Than Allegory (2016)

School has always been a fun place to meet friends, but what its actual purpose is, I never quite understood. "If test scores are so important, why are we all doing the same thing with a class full of different people?", I thought. It took a while, but eventually I found a solution to it. Or rather, I found a new myth for it.

When I was twenty, I learned a lot about learning outside of the educational system. I was completely overwhelmed by the idea that so much was known about this and that I'd never heard about it before. That same year someone asked me what I was good at and, again, I was overwhelmed by the idea that I had no answer to this question and that nobody had ever even asked me this before. It set me on the path of personal development and self-knowledge. The process of obtaining self-knowledge turned out to be the same as the process of getting better at learning. Both are about remembering who you are and remaining open about it. That became the original idea for my first organization: Remind Learning.

We had a program for 15 to 18-year-olds focused on obtaining more self-knowledge by experimenting with smart learning techniques. Doing homework as a means to learn how to take your life into your own hands. These 15 to 18-year-old students passed this on as they tutored 12 to 14-year-olds, and we also trained teachers and parents.

For schools this was interesting because it was about homework, for students it was interesting because it was about themselves. Those in charge of the program were all 20 to 25-year-olds, including myself, and it all worked wonderfully.

The context was different during the training activities and therefore the experience was also different than a "normal" day at school. It was no longer about the content, but about your own experience. "How do you learn now, and how would you like to do it differently? How are you creative? What are you naturally motivated for? What suits you?" It's a phenomenological approach. It's not about giving any specific answers, but allowing people to experience what emerges naturally and help them to make up their own minds.

It's about changing their paradigms by providing a new, intense experience in regards to what school is all about. Therefore, the implicit story changed. It was no longer about test scores and social ability as the central ideas of success, but rather the degree of ownership students experience over their own learning and lives. It was no longer about being concerned with proving how intelligent you are, but discovering in what ways you are intelligent.

With this new context, personalized education became possible, without changing the organization at school.

No laptops, new timetables, or smaller classes are needed for this. By providing an intense experience, a different way of interacting, and celebrating different things together, a new myth emerges. And from that new myth a new organization emerges in a natural way. You don't design a transformation, it happens when you focus on what is real.

The key is not to jump to solutions, but focusing on reconnecting with what is real. What is real is a source of ownership. If we recognize in ourselves: "Yes, this is me!", then personal development is already there before a solution for it is implemented. If you start from the idea that our imagined reality adapts to reality, instead of trying to manipulate reality into our imagination, personal- and organizational change is lightning fast and fun. If you expect people to change their myth after an organizational change, it is often hard work and frustrating. Therefore, most organizational change is done backwards.

By combining homework and self-knowledge, schools were able to begin personalized education before changing anything about the organization. Though it didn't work for everyone. For some, it's still about doing homework in a clever or fun way, and achieving success in the old paradigm. If so, there will be no new, intense experience with schoolwork, and therefore no new paradigm.

You cannot force the transformation of a myth. What you can do is create an environment in which a new connection with reality can occur.

A person's myth is their own sacred ground. The entrance to that sacred ground is only accessible through that specific person. A certain context might help some people, but it varies from person to person. What ultimately works is personal. A person decides for him or herself who and what comes into their heart and becomes part of their myth. Therefore you can never force a new myth to occur. At best, you can provide the space in which a new myth can emerge, because only then will you know if it fits the reality of the specific individuals who are present. We don't need to recondition people, we need to open more space focused on reconnecting with reality.

At one school it took seven years. Seven years of training and trying out different forms until finally, for no apparent reason, a new space was collectively entered. As if by itself, an organization was set up so that Remind was no longer needed. It really doesn't get any better than that.

The effect of a myth was also easy to see within Remind itself. When starting your own business, you see how quickly a myth of a group emerges. You can't control a myth, but everyone influences it. And as an entrepreneur, you see this happen right in front of your eyes.

For instance, at the opening of our first office. You give a speech, everyone drinks your booze and chats with each other and then goes back home. Yet everyone who was there has their own interpretation of what Remind stands for and what it's like to be a part of it. Everyone does this in their own way, because everyone has a different starting point, but their perspectives clearly overlap. The organization grows into its own myth, its own personality that is separate from the people who are a part of it and which makes certain behavior feel either logical or illogical.

Not only do people live in a myth, paradigm and ego, groups of people do as well.

Systems of trust

My inspiration to read fairy tales for this book came from Robert Bly, an American poet and writer. He wrote a book entitled *Iron John* in the 1990s intended to break free from the myth that the macho and domineering man is a mature and developed adult. Using a folk tale from the Brothers Grimm, *Iron John*, as a metaphor, he describes the steps involved in the process of a boy becoming a mature man. Bly does not define what he considers a mature man, but discusses at length the significance of the steps leading up to it. I've never cried over a book before, but this book made me weep several times.

Because Bly describes only the initiations in the process toward becoming mature, I became increasingly aware of the existence of my own unconscious idea of masculinity, as well as my idea of what constitutes maturity. Therefore, I was not given a new story about how a grown man should behave, but became aware of my own myth about mature masculinity. Reading the book was like walking through a gate, it made me step into the unknown. So I understood it is possible to change myths without reprogramming oneself. Transformation is indeed possible.

Obviously, there are also equivalents of *Iron John* for women's maturity process, including the book *Women Who Run with the Wolves* by Clarissa Pinkola Estés. She uses several fairy tales to describe the initiations into mature femininity. The focus and word choice are different from *Iron John*, but the initiations in the process are mostly the same. Masculinity and femininity are opposites, but apparently they have similar initiations on their way to maturity. In my experience, they also have very similar behavior and qualities once they are mature.

Bly and Estés both write with great reverence about people who are able to mature. They describe them as people who have had the courage to search for life's hidden treasures and have found them. In my words: They're people who have mastered the distinction between what is real and what we make real, and know how to prioritize the real things.

Estés also conveys the message that you develop the qualities of mature femininity by becoming aware of your own myth and not by adding a story of how things should be. Estés calls this listening to the river below the river, her description of the myth, the implicit story.

After reading both books, I learned that being mature is about ceasing to put your ego first, your myth. Mature people give their talent unconditionally and inexhaustibly for something greater than themselves. Not in an altruistic way, as if they are not part of it, but in a way they become fully present in the current moment.

This idea also fits well with a new paradigm for sustainability. My study had different courses at different faculties in the university and there you quickly learn different sciences have their own little bubbles. Different ideas about what is a truth, a proof and different definitions of the same thing. For example, in ecology, the Anthropocene era means the era of a world where people are the dominant species. In psychology, the Anthropocene era means a world of people that revolves around people. Subtle difference, but if we combine both, the question becomes: Can we make a world full of people not revolve around people? Or, in other words, can we mature as a human race?

Accelerating sustainability means maturing and helping other people mature (stop prioritizing what we make real over things that are real) while we do the usual stuff like lowering our CO_2 levels, stop using plastics for unnecessary things and erase inequalities.

In his 2015 TED Talk, historian Yuval Harari explains that we live in a world full of people because people can work together flexibly and on a large scale. No other organism can do that. Some can cooperate flexibly, others can cooperate on a large scale. Humans are able to combine the two.

We can do this because we work together in an imagined reality. When we work together, we share a myth, we share an idea of what reality is about. Thereby we pool and focus the time and qualities of the people in a group. To do this, we don't even need to know everyone in the group. As long as we trust the same myth, we can work together.

No one has ever spoken to an organization, or a family, the only thing you can speak to is a person speaking on behalf of an organization or on behalf of a family. Yet every organization and every family has its own characteristics that are separate from the individuals who are a part of it. As if the group had its own personality. This is the effect of our myth, paradigm and ego. A nation, organization and a family system are not real, we make them real.

It's our greatest power and the reason we have become the dominant species on the planet. Influencing everything. The downside of it is that it distorts our idea of what is important in life. If we become too concerned with the myth we share with others, then we perceive less of the reality we share with others. We no longer smell air pollution, we no longer notice when our bodies are too tired to work, we no longer see what our loved ones need and we fail to spend time on what we know is important. By participating in the shared myth, we unintentionally prioritize the myth over that which we know deserves our priority. Myth trumps reality with frightening ease.

"We're more afraid of public speaking than texting on the highway, more afraid of approaching an attractive stranger in a bar than marrying the wrong person, more afraid of not being able to afford the same lifestyle as our friends than spending 50 years in a meaningless career - all because of embarrassment, rejection, and not fitting in really sucked for hunters and gatherers."

Tim Urban, blogger at WaitButWhy

We now live in a world full of humans and we have shown that humanity can coorporate on a global scale. Humanity trusts the myth of money and therefore we can pay with money anywhere in the world. Humanity trusts the myth of a country, of education and of language. Global myths that humanity trusts as a whole exist almost everywhere now.

If there is anything inspiring about today's world, here it lies. All of humanity works together based on something that cannot be described and exists only in our imagination. It's the power of humans.

By sharing a myth, people do not have to wait for DNA adjustments before we adjust to our environment. We can adapt to our environment by adapting the myth we live by. Humans are capable of transforming collectively at lightning speed as we have often done in the past. Especially when we experience a direct life-threatening situation collectively.

What our response to global crises needs is precisely what makes us human. Although the current myth about humans is that people are unwilling or unable to change, reality shows us this is untrue: our myth is the very reason we can create a realistic response to the current global crises. Our ability to create an imagined reality is both our biggest obstacle and our biggest hope.

> *"Ever since the cognitive revolution, Sapiens have thus been living in a dual reality. On the one hand the objective reality of rivers, trees and lions; and on the other hand the imagined reality of gods, nations and corporations. As time went by, the imagined reality became ever more powerful, so that today the very survival of rivers, trees and lions depends on the grace of imagined entities such as the United States and Google."*
>
> Yuval Harari, Sapiens (2017)

In order to learn how to distinguish what is real and what we make real, it helps to have a language for it. What we make real consists of four dimensions that work together in a system of trust and which constitutes our idea of what is normal. Our paradigm is one of them and the most important one. Our paradigm gives the other three their meaning.

First, there's an *original idea* about what is normal. For example, at Remind the original idea is to help students change the myth of learning for tests into learning to improving their self-knowledge. An original idea embodies the meaning of the shared myth for reality.

After the original idea, there's a *soft system*. The soft system consists of symbols and rituals that represent a culture, which has a big influence on people's interpretations of reality. For example, in a company, we might have a logo, a name, an explicit story about the company, perhaps a ritual at lunch and a ritual for the first day of work for new employees.

The soft system points to the myth, like road signs guide traffic. If we change it, people literally get lost. Something as simple as a handshake can greatly affect our interpretation of a person when we first get to know them. If we change our myth, changing our soft system becomes logical. Just like during the pandemic, when everybody understood why shaking hands wasn't advisable anymore, the practice disappeared within days on a global scale.

After a soft system has been established, the *hard system* forms. This system makes following the myth easy and resisting it very difficult. This system is formed by rules, formal hierarchy in an organization, documents and agreements with others, but also roads for traffic, or the laws of a country. The hard system consists of technology and legislation that facilitate a myth, a shared idea about what is normal.

The terms soft and hard systems might be a bit misleading. Our soft system impacts our behavior more than the hard system. The myth, the language of our hearts, sticks more to rituals and symbols than to technology and rules.

If I try to create an image to represent this, I see the original idea of the trust system as a source of water in the mountains from which a river slowly emerges on the way down. The soft system is the river bedding, it guides the flowing water. The hard system is the technology and policies that keep the river safe and usable for people. What is normal is the flowing river and the myth is your interpretation of this picture. It's the river below the river, it determines how we interpret the world and it dictates how we behave.

In a healthy trust system, these four domains fit together and flow in the same direction. There's a lot of work to do in the world if we want to keep the existing trust systems in a healthy state. For instance, the media continuing to share truthful information, politicians continuing to represent citizens, and families and schools providing a safe environment for children to grow up in. Many people are already working on keeping trust systems in a healthy state. And within their system, it's about reconnecting the shared myth with reality.

The special thing about today's global crises is that, even if all current systems of trust are healthy, global crises will still become worse. As there is no trust system for the whole, for the planet, for reality itself, we only have trust systems for parts of reality in our modern world. Mistakenly assuming if all parts are doing their job, the whole will be taken care of.

The reality of today is no longer the reality in which the existing systems originated. A world full of people is a new reality. Following the original ideas of all the current systems is no longer sufficient as a realistic response to global crises. So we need more than healthy, ethical and fair systems of trust. We need to reconnect with reality, starting from the whole, instead of starting with the parts. We cannot work from the parts we have today in order to attain a healthy whole. We thought we could. We were wrong.

The systems we trust, which no longer fit reality, have become castles in the air. They can continue to function if enough people continue to put their trust in them. The system no longer organizes reality as it was intended, or in accordance to reality's needs. The global crises are the result.

Making money with money is a good example of a castle in the air. Money is meant to facilitate the exchange of value between people. Making money with complicated financial products does not do that. Therefore, the money system and the economy can both grow, without adding any value to reality. The castle in the air grows, all our indicators for success grow, but reality doesn't get any better.

If the system we trust has become a castle in the air, then making it healthy is optimizing the wrong thing. So we end up improving something that should not be improved at all. It's just going to do the wrong thing more efficiently. In order to recognize a castle in the air, it's essential we no longer see our own imagined reality as reality. Therefore, the people living outside of a trust system are often the best people to identify a castle in the air. People who are part of the system see their trust system as reality. That's what our myths do, they alter our idea about what is important and hypnotize us into believing our imagined reality is reality. Saying non sensical stuff like: "that's just how it works."

> "People are wonderful. I love individuals. I hate groups of people. I hate a group of people with a 'common purpose'. 'Cause pretty soon they have little hats. And armbands. And fight songs. And a list of people they're going to visit at 3am. So, I dislike and despise groups of people but I love individuals. Every person you look at; you can see the universe in their eyes, if you're really looking."
>
> George Carlin, comedian

Mature people understand that their idea of reality is only a part of reality. They know there is something bigger than their perception. The place where truth, compassion and wisdom live. Mature people can bring these castles in the air down to the ground. They have the courage to regularly walk through the gate, step into the unknown and reassess whether the system they trust in is still working for reality or exploiting it.

The challenge of grounding systems in reality is that the people who are better positioned within the shared myth also get to lead and hold power within the system. Which makes sense because the myth defines our perspective on social status, success and progress. Those who best follow the shared myth get the reward of the group.

Looking beyond a myth is difficult for everyone. After all, everything is a perspective, and that is only reinforced when your environment rewards you for it without question. Success and social status according to the shared myth therefore become a major obstacle in walking through the gate into the unknown and allowing a transformation to occur. In the same way maturing is particularly difficult for 'smart' and 'successful' people. They do not want to step out of their myth and walk through the gate. Because this requires acknowledging that any 'success' is based on a myth.

For Palace people it's extremely difficult to stay connected to reality. Because they test their own imagined reality on yet another made-up system. The economy, politics, the consulting sector and the legal system being the easiest examples. The people in those systems test their success and failure on a made-up system and they pretend it's an objective fact. A 'growing' economy ignores the fact that the economy is made real in the first place, including what we define as 'growing'.

City people live a lot closer to reality. A plumber, a gardener, a farmer and a doctor see reality while they work. In these cases, reality, that which is independent of our trust, is experienced by the person who works in it. Reality is more difficult to ignore for them.

The modern world adds to this difficulty by making our made-up systems so complicated that you first need to study them and master them, before people will even listen to you. But it's very hard to study them and master them without becoming a part of them. Once again, our myths, paradigm and ego make us believe our imagined reality is reality. Therefore, theoretically educated people need plenty of extra help in reconnecting with reality.

People with power and social status are in the best position to keep trust systems connected to reality, but these people have the hardest time in doing exactly that. The more successful and educated you are, the harder it is to accept the fact that reality is always bigger than your imagined reality. It means you have to accept that success is very dependent on how you look at things and, in the end, you might not be as 'self-made' as you'd like to think.

"Greatness is a transitory experience. It is never consistent. It depends in part upon the myth-making imagination of humankind. The person who experiences greatness must have a feeling for the myth he is in. He must reflect what is projected upon him. And he must have a strong sense of the sardonic. This is what uncoupled him from belief in his own pretensions. The sardonic is all that permits him to move within himself. Without this quality, even occasional greatness will destroy a man."

Frank Herbert, Dune (1965)

I had never read a story about colonizing a land from the perspective of an indigenous person. It's such an unbelievable idea to have someone come, take your land and tell you how life works. In the book The Story of Earth - Indigenous Peoples Speaking About Environment and Development (1992), chief Nathan Wate shares his experience.

"Our nature, our environment was in balance. We caught more than enough fish in the lagoon. In our gardens we had an abundance of sweet potatoes, taro, yams, pana, bananas, papayas and leafy vegetables. In the forest we hunted wild boar and birds. We had everything we needed. We worshiped the spirits of our ancestors. We said our prayers as we were used to doing and many of our rituals were closely related to our ancestors and nature. We said prayers before we planted our homesteads. We said prayers before we went hunting. We said prayers before we went fishing. And we had a very special bond with the sharks because we believed that the spirits of our ancestors lived in them. We were never allowed to kill them. We knew their names. We called them to feed them pieces of wild boar. We called them when we were in danger at sea and they would come to our aid.

Everything was in balance. Our prayers, our rituals, our ancestors and nature. We always felt that if the balance was disturbed, everything would change. Therefore, it was necessary to maintain our prayers and rituals. Then the white Christians came, about 90 years ago. From then on, everything began to change. We were told that worshiping the spirits of our ancestors was wrong. The white people told us to worship only our creator. And only in the way the white people did. We had always known that there was a creator, but we did not know him. Our ancestors were related to him. Our ancestors knew who he was. And through our ancestors we were related to him. So we had always left it to the spirits of our ancestors to keep in touch with him. The white people told us all kinds of different things. We got all confused. We didn't know what to believe anymore.

We noticed that the whites had a lot of power. They possessed so many things that we did not have and that we had never seen or known before. So we thought, the white man is so powerful and rich and the white man also knows so much, maybe he is right about the spirits too. We became afraid because the white people also told us stories about heaven and hell, and horrible punishments. All those stories made us terrified and confused. We were no longer allowed to do the things we considered absolutely necessary to maintain balance. For example, we were headhunters. We kept the skulls of our slain enemies in very special and sacred places. Having skulls of our enemies made us strong and helped us to uphold the traditions of our ancestors. We needed skulls to offer sacrifices to our ancestors that respected traditional morals and customs. And since our ancestors helped keep nature in balance, we had to do the things our ancestors wanted us to do. That was wrong, the white man said. Then our headhunting came to an end. But now we think this was the beginning of all the changes and all the problems we now face.

Gradually we forgot our traditional prayers and rituals. The men of our tribes who possessed special knowledge about magic and certain ceremonies no longer passed that knowledge on to the younger people for fear that the whites would get angry. And so young men never learned the customs we had thought for generations were the right ones. The things we believed in changed, our customs changed, and from then on nature began to change as well. Slowly at first... the last 20 or 30 years enormously fast and profoundly. Our population began to increase. Many of our children used to die shortly after birth. We consider that to be the wish of the spirits. The white man brought what he called health care to our islands and the children lived. The people of our tribes are also growing older today, thanks to the knowledge and care of the white man.

Our population has grown, but our land has not. Coastal lands and trees completely occupy all the land we have.

In the old days, we could always alternate and plant new boarding grounds every few years so that the soil of the old boarding grounds could become vigorous and fertile again. In the early days we could also plant many different crops: taro here, sweet potatoes there and a little further yams. Now we can only plant rao or yams or sweet potatoes because the pressure on our soil has become too great. And if we have to give our rangelands a rest, we can't plant anything. Then we have to buy food. But how do we get the money? We cannot take possession of new land because the land adjacent to ours belongs to other tribes who are facing the same problems as we are. When we had enough land, we had large forests. There we went hunting for wild boar and birds. But we had to cut down the forests to build up boarding land. So the wild boars and birds disappeared. Our ancestors had an abundance of fish here in the lagoon. Red sea bass, bream, cod, mackerel, big tuna, bonito or small tuna, mullet, cuttlefish, parrotfish, wahoo. But now we find fewer and fewer of those fish in our lagoon. We have to go outside the coral reef to catch them. But our boats and our fishing gear are not suitable to do that. Moreover, fish are becoming scarce, even outside the reef. What is the reason for this? Have we been fishing too much? Has the environment really changed that much? Are there different sea currents now? And if so, how come? We can't explain it. We know that there are large floating fish factories from a number of countries in the vast ocean. Sometimes we hear stories about big boats from those countries fishing in our waters. They seem to use methods that we don't know about. We have never seen them but we know they catch a lot of fish. Could it be that they are depleting our waters? We have heard that our government has made objections to their fishing practices. In vain it seems. We are a small country, who will listen to us? We have also heard about atomic bombs detonated in the vast ocean. We know nothing about that either, but we have heard that those bombs can destroy people and nature. Why do they do that? The white man told us about the creator who created everything. He told us that killing our enemies for their skulls was wrong. He told us about peace. So why is he making bombs that can destroy everything the creator created?"

I think Nathan Wate's story is a great example of how to tell a story based on things that are real. The book is full of these kinds of experiences from indigenous people from all over the world. To provide a little more perspective, Nathan is still alive today. He is speaking about our own time in history.

Colonizing myths

The amazing thing about a myth is that it allows us to cooperate on a large scale in a flexible way. It's the power of humans. The ugly thing about a myth is that it allows us to colonize land and colonize myths thinking it is progress.

Colonizing land is still happening in some places in the world, and is widely condemned. But colonizing myths happens everywhere, everyday and people are mostly unaware of it. To colonize myths is to force someone or something else to participate in your own imagined reality.

A myth with the belief that it knows what is good for someone else is highly prone to colonizing. A person who trusts his own imagined reality so deeply that he no longer tries to listen to anyone else's reality. This can go so far that colonizing is done out of a belief that it's love. "I love you, this is best for you, therefore I'm doing this for you." Love without connection is as much a castle in the air as money without value is.

Whenever there is no awareness of the reality of those present, there is a colonizing myth. Your imagined reality is then occupied by someone else's. That makes the LGBT+ community, immigrants, indigenous people and former addicts the experts in dealing with a colonizing myth. They could be the leading examples in learning how to start acting from reality and not from our imagined realities. Although sometimes, they become colonizers themselves. Being overly sure about their own ideas.

Myths are different for everyone. We all have different pasts and different conditioning. But there is somewhat of an overlap when people work together. After all, we all trust the idea of money, countries, corporations and education, so at the very least we have those concepts ingrained in our imagined realities.

The modern myth is the shared myth that is dominant now. It's the reason for all the qualities of modern life, therefore it's the biggest obstacle for doing anything meaningful about the current situation of global crisis.

By definition, "developed countries" are the best example of the modern myth, because our idea of development comes from our myth. The modern myth is the shared myth in the modern world. That myth consists, among other things, of an idea about development and progress that is now followed by almost every country in the world.

The modern myth is a myth of 'doing'. Being busy as something worth striving for. The importance of having a goal and a plan to achieve it is a part of this modern myth. As is the pursuit of control to execute the plan as projected. This all follows the idea of success that if we manage to manipulate reality to fit into our story, we will be happy and fulfilled. Predicting the future is therefore a key requirement.

"What's your goal? What's your plan? What are you going to do?"

The modern myth takes a reductionist approach to both knowledge and truth. It's centered around the idea that everything can be understood if you just know its parts. Therefore it constructs the whole based on the sum of its parts. So the world would work in a causal way: everything would have a cause and an effect. It views life as one big complicated machine whose environment determines the outcome; deterministic in its understanding. Therefore, the modern myth ignores the existence of a myth. It ignores that anything inside determines our view on reality.

If something doesn't work, then the modern myth just needs to add something to solve it. For instance, the extra supervision of banks after the financial crisis, intended to prevent the next crisis. That leaves the myth in the financial sector intact, therefore the cause of the crisis is still there, waiting. Or if we get sick we just add medicine or have surgery. And if we experience burnout, we just add treatment until we are back to our old self. Or, in response to the climate crisis, we simply add solar panels and electric cars. The modern myth considers something a solution if it allows what is familiar to continue. The grand vision of our modern world is "to continue". If anything, sustainability needs more ambitions.

Adding something gets in the way of changing the myth, because it quickly appears that adding something is enough. For example, electric cars get in the way of working on a sustainable mobility system. As an object, it solves a bit of the problem, but if you intend to improve the system it really turns out to be an obstacle. It increases mining, increases waste and increases inequalities. It also gives the illusion we're already doing good, while electric cars are nowhere close to being a realistic reaction.

In the modern world we strive to make the imagined reality we live in more beautiful, but what also happens is that we increasingly make it more of a castle in the air. We forget to connect the system we trust with reality itself.

The madness of the modern myth is also evident in our views of maturity. We become adults when we turn 18 years old, but there are other materializations for maturity such as financial independence, knowing a lot about a certain subject, making more and more money, having a steady job, being able to build valuable relationships, having a steady romantic relationship, starting a family of your own, and having children who aspire to accomplish this same list of maturity requirements. The myth is that we mature as we conform to these soft and hard systems. That is, excelling in what others consider normal.

You can meet this entire list and still only be concerned with your own system of trust. Better yet, this myth and this list about being mature encourages you to be preoccupied with your own system and making sure you're separated from reality.

Furthermore, it's a list that can be reached from the outside. None of the things on this list are about character, impact on others, or ethics. This fits in perfectly with a myth that views life as a complicated machine. The modern myth of being mature is about putting your own systems of trust first, which is nothing less than insane. We can't live without others, or our environment. This does make sense, however, in a world full of people that revolves around people. And it explains why the wide range of leaders and followers trust castles in the air over reality. We have our priorities backwards.

We have the same shared myth at the center of the modern world. We inadvertently prioritize familiar trust systems over reality. As a result, when it comes to something we think is very important, we prefer to protect our familiar story more instead of trusting life more. Our core idea on life is that we feel safe because of our myth. We think we only survive because of our myth. So when we think something is important we try to colonize other people's minds *more* instead of opening up more. Thinking it is love.

A good example of this is how parents raise their children. I guess most parents think their children are 'the most important thing in the world'. But most of them aren't very good at listening to their children. Most parents think they know what is best for their children and just want them to behave as they see fit. Which makes sense until they are about 7 years old. Afterwards, their focus should be mainly in listening and showing them what maturity looks like instead of telling them what is good for them, or how the world works.

When we think something is important we put what we know at the center. As a result, we close off our mind and protect our imagined reality even more. In these situations, we don't allow ourselves to have a limited perspective on reality and be vulnerable. The modern myth is a closed myth. A myth that has forgotten that it's a myth. Making us live in a self-conforming bubble.

If people become a parent it would make sense they start to prioritize the whole more and start caring for the environment more. As their unlimited love for their newborn is opening up their hearts to the future of their child. The past decades have shown that usually the opposite happens. When something feels important we look for the power of people, the shared story. When we love something we try to manipulate reality more to fit our story, instead of the other way around. In the modern world most people live for love, not from love. Unfortunately, the sustainability movement shows much of the same mistake.

The urgency of all the global crises combined with the belief that we are running in the wrong direction is exactly why the myth of people in the sustainability movement is also closed most of the time. They feel validated by what they see in reality, but their reaction replicates the problem in their solution. Namely, being sure of how things should be. Once again, the sustainability movement provides a solution just by adding something. Doing even more. Planning even more. Seeking even more control. Knowing what is good for others. The sustainability paradigm has a lot of similarities with the modern paradigm it is trying to change. Closed myths quickly start colonizing other people's imagined realities. This is how we create global crises that no one intended, but happen nonetheless.

We become what we fight against.

The Wizard and Prophet myths do this too. People who trust in one of the stories are mostly convinced that the "other" must be defeated before their solution can really work. The technocracy of the Wizards must be broken according to the Prophets while the soft dreamers must learn how the 'real' world works according to the Wizards. They also believe, like Palace people, that deep down most people want to be exactly like them. And so they both miss the point that they are colonizing myths. We no longer learn from our environment, we no longer see that we are our environment. So we seek ways to use and abuse the environment in order to validate the myth we trust in.

Trying to convince others is not accelerating sustainability. When we convince someone, nothing has improved. At best, someone's imagined reality has become slightly improved. What is needed is not convincing, but healing. What happens when we reconnect with what is real in the world.

The current myth tells us it's logical to feed 60 billion animals, but not 7.9 billion people. It tells us it's logical to give wealthy companies financial support during a crisis, but not to help out people when they are in a crisis. It lets a pension fund think it's logical to invest in fossil fuels and guns, in order to be 'safe for the future'. And it makes people worried about abortions, but not about health care for all. Common sense knows all of this is inconsistent, but we do it anyway because of our myth. And we're all a part of it. Including people who fight it, like myself.

> *"Religion is at its best when it makes us ask hard questions of ourselves. It is at its worst when it eludes us into thinking we have all the answers for everybody else."*
>
> Archibald McLeish, poet

Trying to get on the train before everybody has a chance to get off, is logical for the person who is doing it. Everybody who tries to get off the train finds the person blocking the entrance very annoying, but they're also a part of the problem by politely walking around the person, or worse, telling the person to piss off. We all think we are doing the right thing, but we separate ourselves from the whole in doing so. We all live based on our myth, a made-up story about how the world should be. Only when we completely step out of it and learn to perceive what happens from a distance, can we start reconnecting with reality.

What sustainability needs is more mature people. People

who take responsibility for the whole, who integrates the self, the group and the whole, instead of separating them. Mature people who show us how to put reality first and make sure that our collective imagined reality is actually making reality better.

The young don't have the resources or the time to really do something about sustainability. They are, or should be, busy with discovering their individuality, the world, love, friendship, life, death. Asking the young to stand up for the whole is another example of how things are completely backwards in the modern world. Similarly, young adults are completely overwhelmed with career plans and raising children. Giving them very little room to step back and reconnect with what is real. The biggest resource we don't use for reconnecting with reality are our seniors, the retired, the elders of our communities.

Retirement was never intended for us to dedicate a quarter of our lives to leisure time. The original idea was a few years of rest after a lifetime of physical work. Our seniors have the time, the money and the experience to show us what maturity looks like. They are outside of the system, so it's easier for them to escape the hypnosis of our collective myth. And they don't have the distractions of needing to earn money, defending their ego, or claiming their place in society. The seniors, our elders, could be the face of the acceleration sustainability desperately needs.

Elders can show us what healing looks like. What feeling looks like. What being mature in this world looks like. What reality looks like and why youngsters shouldn't be scared of stepping into the unknown. Elders are in the perfect position to Embody Reality and help humanity step out of its ego.

We separate the young from reality in an artificial reality called education. We separate adults from reality in an artificial reality called careers and family. We separate seniors from reality by acting as if retirement means 'you're out'. Nobody is out of reality. If anybody has the responsibility to start fighting for the whole over the parts, it's our elders.

Letting go of an old myth is the same kind of liberation you can feel after a near-death experience, or any other crisis or trauma. It's better to have a real life than a busy life preoccupied with upholding a story that doesn't really reflect you. It all begins with understanding we are the problem, not the climate, biodiversity or plastic. We are all blocking the exit of a busy train because we want to get in. Not seeing that we are hurting the whole by doing so. To see the whole again and realize we're all blocking the exit is to understand we all walk in two worlds.

I recognize the problem of bringing the two worlds together in my daily life as well. I am more concerned with whether I am sleeping eight hours a night than whether I'm actually tired. And when I'm tired, I often think my plan is more important than going to bed on time. I'm also more concerned with exercising four times a week than checking my body before exercising to see if it's ready for exercise. I eat when it's time to eat, not because I'm hungry. My life has become a smart algorithm instead of actually experiencing what is happening. My own myth of being healthy has become the focus, not my health. Keeping my myth focused on serving reality and not the other way around is hard work. It feels like working on an addiction.

> *"There is often a debate about whether you are part of the problem or part of the solution. My belief is that you can't be part of the solution until you understand that you are part of the problem."*
>
> Mark Tigchelaar, Ocean sailor

Part II
Trusting life

My most literal experience of walking through a gateway to a new reality was when I walked through the gate of a Zen garden in Japan. Here I truly stepped into another world. A Zen garden is designed to mimic the power of nature and make it accessible for people. Sitting by the garden and looking at it is designed to be the ideal environment for contemplation and meditation. They can be found in city parks, near temples and at old manor houses.

The art of creating Zen gardens is described in the book Sakuteiki, which literally means "setting stones". It's the oldest book on gardening in the world and is filled with timeless wisdom such as, "Don't put the stone upside down" and "Water flows in through the north, bends to the east and leaves the garden in the west." It's like the Chinese classic Art of War by Sun Tzu, but for gardening.

The most famous Zen garden is in Kyoto and is called Ryoan-ji. It has fifteen large stones laid out in a rectangular field of carefully raked pebbles. The large stones are positioned in such a fashion that from every angle only fourteen can be seen while one remains hidden. The mystery of life is always just beyond what is visible.

You walk through the gate at the entrance and you step into another world. It had a similar feeling of visiting a museum. Everyone is walking with a leaflet in their hand and only whisper when speaking to one another. However, it is an open place. The bed of pebbles is surrounded by walls, but the sound of the city around it can be clearly heard.

I was in Japan to study Zen gardens. I had read the book and it had touched me deeply, but nowhere did it say what you do when visiting one. I just sat down on the steps on the long side of the garden. There were a lot of people, it was high summer and it was sweltering hot, so I put in my earplugs and turned on the sound of rain in my meditation app.

As I sat there, the following question came up: What is it that I see? It came without requiring an answer. It was more like an invitation to let the light fall into my eyes and silence arise in my being. When thoughts came forth, I repeated the question: What is it that I see? Sometimes I looked at the details, but mostly the image of the whole came to me. I think the stillness induced a trance, because the static image of a pebble bed full of large stones moved several times. The richness and vibrancy that emerged was incredible. I also got a glimpse of the missing fifteenth stone without being able to see it from where I was sitting. When I looked at my phone again, three hours had passed.

Examining reality with the question "What is it that I see?" pierced through my myth. I no longer saw what I expected to see, but I allowed the image of the garden to emerge. It brought me to the realization that reality is the most concrete world there is, yet it can never be fully described. It's the world that astronauts see from space and that we wake up in every morning. It's the world where national borders do not exist and judgments and expectations do not occur. Yet it cannot be described through language. Every expression of reality is an imagined reality, a filter over what it truly is. Even though reality is the most concrete thing there is, it is unfathomable, unintelligible and impossible to describe. It can only be experienced, and only if we're not hypnotized by our myth and our idea of how life is supposed to be.

The experience at Ryoan-ji inspired me to meditate more often with my eyes open and connect with the place where I am. There were also beautiful places in the city where I lived, so why not meditate there? For the next four years, I guided meditations at these beautiful locations in the city having connection as a goal. In this way, I created a new trust system, after having a new experience with reality. Within that new imagined reality, other people could experience what is real for themselves at that precise moment. One participant described it as, "I get up with plans for the day and after monking (that's what we called it) those plans are gone and there is only: I'm hungry, let's eat."

Backwards

Our myth, paradigm and ego is the big piece of the pie that we forget in our response to global crises. Those who look for solutions within the modern myth get no further than temporary, partial solutions. However, this doesn't mean that we can simply abandon the old trust systems. Current systems are also the reason for all the good qualities of the modern world. And history shows us that paradigms usually change like Russian Matryoshka dolls. They integrate and include the old, not erase it. As in Europe, the aboriginal, greek and roman temples are often seen adjacent to or even over one another.

Nor is it the goal to live without a myth. That's not possible and it would overlook the fact that sharing a myth is the very power we have as humans, and that we need it for organizing a world full of people.

What does help is to examine what is dependent on our trust, and can therefore be changed, as well as what is not dependent on trust, and is the world we share. From this distinction a table emerged where the left column lists elements belonging to the trust system, which therefore has an original idea, a myth and both soft- and hard systems. The right column shows what part of reality the trust system tries to organize. This is the essence of the trust system. In no particular order.

Imagined reality. *The world we make real*	**Reality.** *The world that is real.*
Friendship, marriage, family system	Love between people
Legal system	Justice
Career	Meaningful work
Flirting, dating	Being in love
Economy	Nature
Money	Value exchange
Woman, Man	Human
Health ideals and rituals	A healthy body
Science, journalism, spirituality	Truth
Education	Learning
Personality	Soul
Democracy	Group of people
Health care	Healthy people
Police	Safety
Nations, United Nations	Planet
Religions	God
Sustainability movement	A sustainable world

If we colonize myths, we put our own imagined reality at the center of the world and exploit reality in order to maintain our imagined reality. That's organizing things backwards. Then, what happens is that you pretend to walk in one world thinking you know reality and what is good for somebody else.

Modern economy has a colonizing myth. The original idea of the economy is to organize natural resources so that everyone has a good household and nature becomes more prosperous. Currently, we have an economy that exploits both natural resources and humans in order to create massive inequality among households. When the system we trust (imagined reality) grows, we think the economy is doing well, when in fact the economy is only doing well when everyone has a good household and nature is becoming more prosperous (reality).

The modern world organizes almost every area of life backwards. We want more money when in fact we seek more value. We seek affirmation for our identity when we actually want to be ourselves. A country wants to organize itself first and only then thinks about a healthy planet. What we make real quickly seems more important than what is real. This builds castles in the air and does not serve reality. And global crises are the result.

Placing what is familiar as the most important thing is the modern myth's main focus. This is why we make decisions that sound logical but are irrational. No countries can exist without a healthy planet. No economy can exist without nature. And you only get trauma from a family without love.

A family system is not that important, love between people is important. A nation, or an economy is not that important. A healthy planet and thriving nature is important. Looking at reality from our imagined reality is like looking in a mirror. By doing this, we can only see the confirmation of our own myth. We can only see a climate crisis when in reality there is nothing wrong with the climate, but what is tremendously wrong is the myth we trust. Our myth is completely backwards, the effect of putting our ego at the centre of the world.

With religions this becomes extra visible. For instance, when we see believers worship a God that stands for all that is, and is the symbol of absolute love, yet believers exclude those who are "different". That's how you know they have their own system at heart and not the essence of their faith. Just like polluting companies are seen as successful if they make a lot of money. Even if they trash the planet and exploit their employees. And we're fine with dishonest politicians as long as a lot of people vote for them. Or freedom fighters who only fight for their freedom. The modern myth puts the system at the center for the system's own sake and therefore loses sight of what is essential, its purpose, its meaning for reality. That's the very definition of being immature.

We have a wrong perspective of the whole. We act as if it is a thing outside of the world of things. Which, of course, is not true. Each thing is part of the world of things, the whole is something else. It is like another dimension. The whole does not exist outside each thing and each thing has the whole reflected in itself.

For example, self-interest based on your own imagined reality means you only (or primarily) take care of what you perceive as yourself. You separate 'self' from the whole. While self-interest from reality means you take care of the whole. Because we are the whole. I do not know any leader or concept that puts reality, the whole, first.

In the past, we had places, ceremonies and rituals, like the Zen gardens I described earlier, that were designed for keeping our priorities straight. What is real is important and primary in life. What we make real we can change and is secondary in life. These old ceremonies created the required mental and physical space for contemplation and meditation in order to access a clear vision on what is real and what we make real. Now we have gone so far from this that we think the column on the left of our table is concrete and the column on the right is vague and abstract. While, of course, it's the other way around. What is real is concrete and robust, like safety, love and the planet. What we make real is abstract and very fragile, like democracy and our legal system.

Nassim Nichlas Taleb tells us that 'robust' is a bad word for things that are real, in his book *Antifragile*. Robust means it doesn't become weaker from external stress. Or, to be completely impervious from outside influence. Like a bridge that can outlast a hurricane. But real things aren't completely impervious, they actually get better from stress. We don't have a word for that, so Taleb called it 'antifragile'. The opposite of fragile. Fragile meaning something weakens with damage. Reality is antifragile, it learns from experience.

The modern myth normalizes the act of inventing a story about the world (left column), then bring it into the world through our inspiration, passion, and talent (right column). Then, it tries to get as many followers as possible to trust our story of what success is (left column). We call it the American Dream and its focus is on manipulating reality.

A more realistic path would be to start with our connection to reality and relive its essence through silence, contemplation, meditation, long walks in nature and prayer (right column), create soft and hard systems for what emerged from reality (left column) and then stay open and connected to what reality is showing you as the effects (right column).

Going Left-Right-Left seems logical, but is backwards, separates you from reality and makes you sure of everything. Going Right-Left-Right is rational and makes you open and connected to everything. The easiest anchor for this is to examine what you measure as success. Is it dependent on a trust system, or is it independent of a trust system?

Being able to distinguish both worlds is essential. This seems easier than it actually is because we see the world through the filter of our perspective. This is the hypnotic effect of our myth and it distorts our idea of what is important in life. So what we experience in the world is mostly our own illusion and not reality as it is. To get out of this dynamic, we often need other people to give us honest, compassionate and direct feedback. Or place ourselves in a completely new context, such as a new hobby, reading a new book, or a new holiday destination. Then, once again, if we have an open myth, we experience that what we consider to be normal is not that normal after all. In summary: *How we experience the world says more about our own myth than what it says about the world itself.*

It helps if we pay attention to everything on the right column of the previous table and the one below. This means experiencing the essence, so that a myth may emerge that is again grounded in what is real.

There are also areas that live in our imagined reality, and areas that belong to reality. These also help us distinguish what serves the different areas of our life in a better way.

Typical for our imagined reality	Typical for reality
Goals	Results
Language	The implicit
Power of humans	Miracle of life
Stories	Meaning
Choices	Decisions
Normal	Natural
Success	Honor
Intelligence	Common sense
Popularity	Integrity
Subjective, objective	Mystery
Do kind things	Be kind
Identity, group identity	Who you are, who we are
Anticipate	Spontaneity, Flow
Skill	Talent
Games	Playing
Willpower	Letting things emerge, unfold
Logic	Rationality

In the two tables I've shared, the column on the right is intangible. And the words will be interpreted differently by everyone. The meaning we give to language is always built on associations, connections and interpretations. Language is a filter over reality and therefore always belongs to our imagined reality. In the same way a feeling is already something before we have a word for it, reality exists before we have a language for it.

This table and this whole book are therefore a good expression of my own myth, and reality remains a puzzle to be solved together. We find the effect of a system in reality and not in a book. Ensuring that we continue to do what is right for reality together means continuously exploring what the essence of reality is together, and whether we are still serving it. It's the reason why the message of this book is in the white spaces of these pages rather than in the black letters.

There is nothing as simple as reversing our perspective and starting from reality. It's focusing on the most concrete, obvious thing. It's right in our face. But, at the same time, there is nothing quite as difficult. Our myth invades all and constantly plays games with our perception. It's as simple as it is difficult.

The hypnosis of our myth and our fear of reality (death) make us prefer to follow the stories of our loved ones rather than what we know to be true. In reality, we also have to face death and all the other things we have learned to turn away from. Facing reality is often very scary.

To organize ourselves based on reality is a transformation of what we trust. It's about trusting life more than trusting the existing systems. Which is very grounding. A grounded system has a myth that continuously adapts to reality. A myth that continuously adapts to reality is an open myth, the opposite of a closed myth. A closed myth lives only in its own imagined reality and is sure of everything. An open myth is imbued with the fact that how we see and experience the world is our own imagined reality and that there is always a larger reality of which we are all a part of.

> *"Two younger fish swim in the ocean, when they happen to come across an older fish, swimming in the opposite direction, who nods at the two young fish saying, "Morning boys, how's the water?" They swim on for a bit until one young fish asks the other: "What the hell is water?"*
>
> David Foster Wallace, philosopher and writer

The tables also reinforce the idea of what maturing looks like. Becoming aware of your own limited perspective of the world also means being open to the larger reality which you are a part of. If we begin to examine the larger reality, we come back to the essence. We soon see that, in the left column, we have very separate systems and stories, but everything in the right column can often be experienced together and simultaneously. In reality everything comes together, in our imagined reality we separate everything from each other. They're completely different dimensions and not opposites.

Keeping the two worlds connected is the function of spirituality, journalism and science. They exist in order to keep our myths about the world open. They're our systems for truth seeking. Spirituality is the most neglected one in this modern world while science and journalism are too often used for proving existing stories. Science and journalism are very dependent on what we want to pay for, and people want to pay for things that confirm their myths.

The myth of journalism is to report neutrally about what happens. Of course, there is no such thing as neutral communication, but it's important to strive for it nonetheless. By stating what is real we can keep our imagined reality connected to reality. When journalists report on corruption, illegal acts of the government, or any other hidden activity, we get a chance to adapt our imagined reality to that information. The essence of journalism is to bring things to light. It's very spiritual and very hard work. Most people don't want to look at the bad things happening in the world and change their imagined realities. Like the black lives matter, metoo, and sustainability movements have proven recent years.

The role of the media during the pandemic is another good example of the power of our myth. If we have a myth that has people at its center (looking for stability, uniformity and keeping the group together), you probably think the media did a great job during the pandemic. They were almost all echoing the message of their government as if there was only one rational way of dealing with the pandemic. Giving you as many arguments as possible for why you are normal and people who thought differently were horrible people. This helped people deal with their fear of death.

If you have a myth that puts what is real at its center, you think the media did a horrible job. Completely missing the point that there were many rational ways to deal with the pandemic. That everything was a choice and nobody knew beforehand which choice was better. So presenting a story as the one and only rational thing is clearly lying.

Now the example is that you cannot explain these two worldviews to people through language. Both groups just see the confirmation of their own story, and talking about it quickly becomes a discussion that polarizes people even more. You don't work on paradigms like you work on technology or legislation or money. It's a new field, in which very, very few people have solid experience in.

The myth of spirituality is that there is no objective outside world where we are separate from. So when we examine the outside world we encounter ourselves. We see the world as our myth. And when we examine our inner world we encounter reality. Spirituality is anything that helps you see past your own perspective and makes you adopt an open, connected, loving way of being.

I know this sounds vague to the modern mind. Just look again at the tables. Everything in the right column lives inside of us. What we try to organize out there with our trust systems is actually in ourselves.

Science and spirituality have the same goal: to get closer to reality. In doing so, science pursues an objective truth and spirituality a subjective one. Science seeks truth in what can be repeatedly observed and what can be logically deduced. Spirituality seeks truth in examining how the world enters us. Because how the world enters us says a lot about our own myth. Therefore, we improve our ability of recognizing what is real and what we make real.

The spiritual path organizes our inner world in a better way, so that we can act from truth in the world and keep our systems of trust grounded. Even if following the truth means going against our own ego, or against our old beliefs. Zen gardens, praying, meditation, ceremony, reading, all of this helps in this regard.

A world full of people needs all three of them. We need the insights of science (we can't go on like this), journalism (it's really happening) and spirituality (we ourselves are the problem in the world). So, it's not surprising that our response to global crises lacks spirituality the most. In the mental landscape of the modern man, spirituality is the driest desert of all.

The gap between our myth and our reality has to become smaller. If we don't do it, the reason to do it will become greater. So it's going to happen, we will reconnect with reality. The greatest contribution you can make to this is to increase your trust in life. Trusting the whole. Adding stories, or solutions will only confuse people even more.

"It takes a special turn of mind to grasp formless reality in its essential nature and to distinguish it from the figments of the imagination which, all the same, thrust themselves urgently upon our attention with a certain semblance of reality."

Johann Wolfgang von Goethe, poet

I studied a BS in Industrial Engineering and Management. In the end I understood that I was learning to manage a factory, which I didn't find very appealing. For my master's I switched to Industrial Ecology. It's a two year research master's about sustainability, which combined subjects and teachers from three different universities in the Netherlands. You learn how to analyze sustainability on a systemic level, from a multi-disciplinary approach and design them as an ecological system. In short, designing human systems as if they were a natural system. I absolutely loved it.

It made me study nature more and visit industries, farms and nature conservation areas where they applied similar designing principles. Focusing on closed loops, clean materials and boosting the regenerative abilities of nature.

Placing what is real as a priority is difficult for people who grew up in a world that revolves around what we make real. Even in areas where the goal is to think of nature as the most important thing, the story is often the most dominant aspect of the equation.

For example, the biodiversity crisis means that, in some places, many different species of plants and animals are put together. But every ecologist knows that the introduction of new species in an ecosystem requires several generations before building symbiotic relationships with each other. Lots of species forced together is not necessarily a healthy ecosystem. So we quickly do it the wrong way around, precisely with the things we consider important.

Similarly, a narrative exists that only native plants and animals are suitable for a certain ecosystem, which is fueled by the observation that invasive species can upset the balance of this ecosystem. Invasive species are plants and animals that, due to increasing globalization, urbanization, and global warming, are spreading faster and faster into ecosystems where they don't really belong, and therefore disrupt things by doing so.

In that narrative of nature restoration, plants and animals that don't belong somewhere are being removed. Which, of course, creates the dilemma that we have to choose which species are original and which are not. But, what time period do you use? Because what is original in nature changes over the millennia.

Even if you know for sure which plants and animals belong somewhere, do they still fit the world of today? You can't protect them from climate change, plastic pollution or bee extinction. The environment has changed since these native plants and animals were native.

This is not to say that invasive species are not a problem. However, the problem is just not solved by simply removing them. Learning to listen to the environment and trusting life is what nature restoration requires. Not another myth about how things should be. As humans, in order to do good, we don't have to follow our preexisting story of what good looks like.

"If we let go of explicit ethics and stay with our natural selves then we are ethical. Living from explicit ethics only leaves us with doubts about whether we are doing the right thing."

Anthony de Mello, writer

Truly listening to nature and following its flow quickly presents the challenge that we don't find it beautiful or useful. Reality can be beautiful and useful, but it can also be ugly and useless. We act as if nature we consider dead is not regenerative and so we want everything to be vibrant, colorful, functional and preferably profitable. All four concepts are myths about how things should be and that is precisely what inhibits nature's regenerative ability instead of enhancing it. You enhance the natural processes that are always there by letting go of wanting something from them. You need to stop colonizing them.

There is a 'rewilding project' at the Knepp Castle Estate in the UK where they put nature in charge of what's needed to be done. The first few years this resulted in an ugly and chaotic natural park that nobody wanted to have anything to do with. Until slowly so many rare animals and plants emerged that the government wanted to apply national rules in order to protect these rare animals and plants. The intention was to force them to make the presence of those rare animals and plants their priority. To which the people of the park replied that those rare animals and plants appeared precisely because no priorities were applied.

Restoring nature where nature is in charge is giving space to the natural processes: nature without people's stories getting in the way. It's trusting the myth that arises from the situation, of which we ourselves are therefore a part of. And that's where it gets interesting: When do you see yourself as part of the situation and when do you put a story over reality? You will never be able to provide an answer with certainty. The only thing that you can do is to keep your story, the left column, in service to something that no one fully understands and can only be experienced, the right column.

My thesis is: If you allow what is in yourself to flow naturally, you can tend to wild nature without taming it. This won't work as long as we are mired in old myths about how the world, or nature, should be.

Of course, we ourselves are also nature and so are our cities. The focus should be in wanting to improve the whole, not the whole minus human beings. Listening to natural processes is not as simple as it sounds. It's more of a life skill than knowledge. It's more about following wisdom than doing intelligent things.

In the Netherlands, where I grew up, there's an area containing four major cities, called the Randstad. It's between 2 and 6 meters below sea level already. The Dutch keep it dry with dikes, pumps and dunes. If the Dutch would listen to their reality, they would see that the ground is subsiding, the groundwater is salinating and the river dikes are no longer enough to contain the water due to the sea level rising. If we prioritize reality in the Randstad, it will undoubtedly mean moving the Randstad. Either we plan to do it, or nature does it for us. Like what is already happening in Jakarta, Venice and Mexico City. In our mind, our myth is a powerful and robust thing, that overwrites reality easily. From the perspective of reality, the things we make real are easily replaceable.

The Dutch fighting the water levels is no longer an engineering marvel and an example for the world. It's turning into a symbol of the modern age's naivete. Trying to control what is real with things that we make real. Living backwards.

Miracle of life

The miracle of life is that everything balances itself. Just like a plant needs the right amounts of light, air, soil and water, and it will grow, bloom and reproduce, and it knows exactly how to do all these things. Well, the same happens when we leave farmland alone from time to time without asking anything of it. Then the natural processes bring the soil back to life.

We organize the power of humans through systems of trust which only live in our imagined reality. The miracle of life is the workings of reality, the workings of the whole.

The miracle of life is what can improve the whole. Something a part can never do. Therefore, the whole is the main focus in order to find a realistic reaction to our global crises. The miracle of life organizes itself and it needs nothing but our trust and presence. The more words we try to attach to the natural processes, or the whole, the more we try to pull something into a system of trust that actually has no language. Natural processes live outside of our perspectives and can only be experienced when we focus on the whole. Also called the Gestalt.

Natural processes can be felt when we take a five-minute break on a busy day and enjoy the sun. Five minutes of alert and relaxed enjoyment of the warmth of the sun transforms our experience of the entire day. When we connect with the things on the right column of the tables shown in the previous chapter, we can feel this effect. Play, nature, spontaniety and health are all effects of this miracle. And we usually experience them all at the same time. The natural processes are everywhere and yet nothing is more easily overlooked.

One of the principles which Hippocrates taught us is there has never been a doctor who has cured a patient. At best, the doctor has created the conditions for the body to heal itself. Just as a therapist has never made a patient feel full of life again. Just as a teacher has never made a student understand anything, and you have never made yourself fall in love, and you have never relaxed yourself. Life is the gift of life. Period.

"Life is what happens.
While we are making other plans."

John Lennon, artist

When we live from this awareness, an enormous joy arises from the simplest things. Seeing a flower, a child that plays, a smile on somebody's face, the taste of a single bite of watermelon during a hot day, a handshake. Everything becomes a miracle. As soon as you realize you're not breathing, you receive breath. So sit back, be amazed, the engine drives the car, you just need to steer once in a while. This is the miracle of life and it brings balance to the whole. All you have to do is not stand in the way with a story about how things should be.

Everything exists thanks to the miracle of life, only in the modern myth do we pretend that everything arises as a result of our actions. This makes it seem as if it's smart to put the modern myth at the center. The myth thereby claims a result that it did not produce.

No matter how difficult an operation in the hospital might be, the body ultimately heals itself. Dating is something we do, but in the end we fall in love naturally, or not at all. No matter how much work raising a child is, in the end it's the child who grows up on his own. Life is much more about creating the right circumstances than it's about doing anything ourselves. Natural processes do the real work. Embracing this requires an earthbound confidence in life. It requires shifting our trust to the larger reality of which our imagined reality is only a part of. It's about trusting the whole rather than trusting our own systems.

In order to assimilate the miracle of life, we need to learn to distinguish when our imagined reality fits reality and when it does not. Every moment, every situation, every person, plant and animal is unique, and there is no way to make sure you're doing the right thing. It's about ceasing to try to improve the world based on our myths and learning to embrace what emerges naturally. It's about learning to see the whole and then the parts. Not trying to construct the whole from the parts up, as we are shown at school and at work.

Seeing our old paradigm as the global crisis will entail doing something different in different places around the world, and so the path to sustainability is going to look different everywhere. There is no absolute "sustainable behavior" or anything like "doing good in the world." That only indicates that you have a closed myth. To let life lead the way means moving out of uniformity and certainty, and instead learning how to live in diversity and uncertainty.

"Wild Geese
You do not have to be good.
You do not have to walk on your knees
for a hundred miles through the desert, repenting.
You only have to let the soft animal of your body
love what it loves.
Tell me about despair, yours, and I will tell you mine.
Meanwhile the world goes on.
Meanwhile the sun and the clear pebbles of the rain
are moving across the landscapes,
over the prairies and the deep trees,
the mountains and the rivers.
Meanwhile the wild geese, high in the veal blue air,
are heading home again.
Whoever you are, no matter how lonely,
the world offers itself to your imagination,
calls to you like the wild geese, harsh and exciting—
over and over announcing your place
in the family of things."

Mary Oliver, poet

It's global crises that teach us where our imagined reality is colonizing reality. Global crises show us where our shared myth is leading to, and that's not closer to reality. Global crises encourage us to relearn how to look at what fits in the world today and what doesn't. If we don't learn this, the need to do it will become ever greater until we open up and we put reality at the center once again. There is absolutely nothing natural about the modern world and it is helping us to let go of it and be open for reality again.

Political radicalization helps us to rethink our myth of politics. Economic stagnation helps us to look at value exchange differently. Meaningless work helps us to re-examine what we want from our work. Natural disasters help us to look differently at how we interact with nature and where we live. The pandemic helped us to see that there are things more important than our plans. In the same way, climate change, mass extinction and the loss of biodiversity help us to rethink what progress looks like, what deserves to be a priority and what being rich means.

Remembering that we ourselves are the global crises and that global crises are an expression of our inner world can only be done with a deep trust in life. By doing this, the end of everything we know is not going to become less probable. And only when we trust in something beyond our current myth can we respond to it without wanting to change it, or worse, to add something to it.

Just as we mature from learning to listen to our own 'river below the river' and not by following a preconceived idea of maturity, we collectively mature from learning to listen to our environment, learning to listen to what is real and learning to trust what emerges.

Global crises are the signposts on the path to a new paradigm. They keep us on the path in order to become a part of life on this planet once again. They are stern teachers, provided we have an open myth and are open to reality. Otherwise they will continue to be the problems of the world that need to be solved. With an open myth we dare to become a part of reality. When we become a part of the global crises we also see how we ourselves are the problem, not someone or something else. That's the effect of reconnecting with reality and the result of the spiritual path.

There is nothing on the planet that stands in the way of a sustainable and equal world full of people except the modern myth, our collective ego. There is nothing wrong with reality, but what's really wrong is what we put our trust in. In this way, humanity can't be viewed as bad, we just trust something that no longer fits reality.

Doing something about the global crises means learning to deal with ourselves. When we let our myth emerge from reality, we lose control over the world, but we start to influence what happens in the world. Therefore, influence arises over things we have no control over. This is the way to a new paradigm for sustainability. This has always been the way for everything.

"The masters of life do not optimize their lives. The masters of life optimize their attitude toward life."

David Deida, The way of the Superior Man (1997)

Our state of being

So far we have discussed the power of humans and the miracle of life as concepts. But they're not just ideas, they are a part of our bodies as well. We embody the two worlds. Psychiatrist and neurologist Iain McGilchrist has dedicated his life to researching our two brain hemispheres and compiled his findings in his two modern classics: *The Master and His Emissary (2009)* and *The Matter with Things (2021)*.

The way he explains it is that our left hemisphere is specialized in representing reality and our right hemisphere is specialized in presenting reality. The left hemisphere is busy with concepts, labels, criteria, abstractions and recordings about what is real. The right hemisphere is busy with: Where am I? What is true? How does this make sense?

Sounds familiar, right?

Most animals have a left and right hemisphere in their brains. Our left hemisphere is optimized for 'eating'. So it's specific, detailed, tool-oriented, focused and reductionist. It tries to construct the whole from the parts up. Making it very easy to leave things out.

Our right hemisphere is optimized for 'not being eaten'. It's focused on the whole and scans it for possible dangers. It sees the whole before the parts.

Now, the research on hemispheres became very popular

very quickly in the 1990s and a lot of nuance got lost during this period. So much so that the current myth is that there is no difference between the hemispheres, because you always use both. Iain McGilchrist shows in his books that there are numerous asymmetries (as he calls it) and problems in different parts of the brain produce very different effects. This indicates they do not have the same role and function. So we use both hemispheres extensively at whatever we do, but there is a clear specialization for each one. And in the modern world we got them backwards. In Iain's words: "Our left hemisphere is a good emissary and a terrible master. In the modern world we listen to the emissary and have forgotten about the master."

Furthermore, both hemispheres can carry consciousness. So, if for some reason, one of the two is not working, you are still conscious of yourself. But they have a very different state of being, as if two different personalities live in our brains, which in healthy people are mixed into one single consciousness.

The metaphor Iain McGilchrist uses to illustrate this is to see our consciousness as an unknown country where two spies are being sent to. Every week one message comes back from one of the two spies about what's going on in the unknown country. After a few months it's clear that one spy is very reliable and the other one, not so much. Unfortunately, it's not immediately clear which spy sends us the message when we receive it. We have to learn to distinguish the different kinds of signals that come our way in order to learn what the qualities of each hemisphere are and when to use them. So what we experience as one consciousness is a mix of two, both of which have very different qualities.

Also, all of our body's movements are controlled by the opposite brain hemisphere. So, for instance, the left hand is getting instructions from the right hemisphere and vice versa. Also, our sight is received in the opposite brain hemisphere. So when one hemisphere is not working, you lose control and sight from the opposite side of your body.

In general, the left hemisphere is occupied with seeking ways to use reality. It knows what is explicit and literal, like words, and sees the world as a collection of parts that work causally together in linear steps. Life, from the left hemisphere's point of view, is seen as a complicated machine. It's busy predicting the future and looking for ways to control and manipulate it. It's confident it knows reality although it only knows labels and criteria. Just a representation of what is real. It thinks it's winter because it's January (for those living in the northern hemisphere), and not because it looked at the trees, for example.

The right hemisphere is occupied with testing our conclusions and actions in reality. It gives us the sense of time and our body's movements. It's busy with seeing the whole and is most useful for creative activities, empathy, intelligence (understanding) and humor. It does not know language, but it's needed in order to understand it within a context. Like understanding memes, for example.

Dead clichés activate the left hemisphere: *all babies are angels*. Alive metaphors activate the right hemisphere: *clouds are pregnant ghosts*.

The body's hardwiring of both hemispheres are mirrors of their specialties. The left is wired with a lot of short connections between brain cells. Whereas the right has long connections, connecting different parts of the hemisphere at once. You can almost feel it while reading the alive metaphor. It needs different parts of the brain to work together in order to understand it.

Because we give our left hemisphere information too much weight, while our right hemisphere knows reality better, it often sounds like the left hemisphere is bad and the right hemisphere is good. That is not true, we need both to function properly.

For example, humans can detect 40 million different colors. Naming them all differently will be very impractical, therefore we need the criteria, abstractions and labels of our left hemisphere to describe them. But we shouldn't forget what they are, abstractions of reality. One color may be blue to some, grey to another and green to a third, all being correct.

> "*In a perfect world the right is the gift of life and the left makes sure what comes as a gift is made serviceable and can be called upon by will.*"
>
> Iain McGilchrist, The Matter With Things (2021)

When we cook a delicious meal with our left hemisphere in the lead, we follow a recipe. When we cook a delicious meal with our right hemisphere in the lead. We taste regularly and what we taste decides what we do next. We use the recipe for what it is: an abstraction and use it as a guideline.

There are far more connections and communication from the right hemisphere to the left hemisphere than from the left to the right. The left lives in its own bubble and it isn't aware it doesn't know reality. It also easily silences the right hemisphere because, as it knows explicit language, it easily overwrites or ignores any input from the right hemisphere. Our right hemisphere is inclusive by nature and knows its limitations. It knows it needs the left hemisphere in order to function properly. Our left hemisphere doesn't know the right hemisphere exists.

For example, our left hemisphere sees only competition in nature and between people and is looking for ways to win. Our right hemisphere knows there is competition and coorporation, empathy and harmony in nature and between people and is looking for ways to understand and integrate it all.

In the words of Iain McGilchrist: "Discovering the differences between the left hemisphere and the right hemisphere is like discovering a new landscape". It takes time and experience. His latest book, *The Matter with Things*, is 3,267 pages long. He shares his conversations with patients, the results of scientific experiments and his own explanations and metaphors to give the reader space to explore this new landscape.

It becomes clear that the hemispheres are very different, although you use them both at all times. Our spies send messages back from both hemispheres all the time. It's up to us to learn to distinguish the two and use them appropriately. The tables in the chapter 'Backwards' indicate clearly we have a lot of rewiring to do.

To highlight the differences Iain McGilchrist gives clear statements about what the patients and experiments have taught him about the hemispheres. Here are a few of his statements to give you an idea of the different hemispheres we use to construct our idea of reality and the different states of being they produce.

Left hemisphere	Right hemisphere
Mechanical	Human
Reductionistic	Whole
Tool awareness	Body awareness
Moves to stasis	Moves to flow
Philosophical, abstract and views the concrete as secondary	Holds perception of time, movement and speed
Grossly overestimates itself and blames others when in trouble	Underestimates itself and blames itself when in trouble
"How can I use this?"	"Where am I?"
Jumps to conclusions	Intuitive insights
Logical	Rational
Closes and seeks closure	Opens and seeks connection
Schizophrenia and autism	Depression
Everything is somewhat familiar	Everything is somewhat new
Explicit motivation from cognitive construct: What do I want?	Implicit motivation from the unconscious: What am I doing when I feel good?
Confabulates	Tests assumptions in reality. Our 'bullshit' detector
Social rivalry and self-regard	Social bonding & empathy
Can't put a narrative together	Understands humor, irony, memes and human motivation
Excels at repetitive tasks and when all required information is present (almost never). Gets worse if you give it more time.	Excels when everything isn't clear or available (almost always). Gets better when there is more time
Used for manipulating the world	Used for understanding the world

Left hemisphere	Right hemisphere
Out-of-body experience and hallucinations	Showing and magnifying beauty in nature
Works from a representation of the world	Works with how the world presents itself
Separated self	Integrated self

> *"The distinction between the two is not just how we think, feel or act about the world. More how we give attention. What shapes our being in the world. Therefore phenomenology is important."*
>
> Iain McGilchrist, The Matter With Things (2021)

Clearly the hemispheres are very different and at the same time very difficult to distinguish in practice. Are you jumping to conclusions or having an intuitive insight? Are you hallucinating or magnifying beauty? Are you logical or rational? Are you separating yourself or integrating yourself? Are you seeking closure or opening up possibilities? Unfortunately, it is not as easy as it sounds. Thankfully, every step you make is very rewarding.

A great deal of the explanations Iain McGilchrist gives for the workings of the hemispheres are studies of people who do not have a proper functioning brain. When parts of the brain do not work anymore we can study what changes in our perception and functioning in reality. For example, here are two exchanges with two patients, recorded by Georg Kerkhoff. Both suffer objective difficulties with reading and visual disturbance. The first one suffers from homonymous hemianopia (right posterior infarction):

> Examiner (E): Have you noticed any changes in your vision since you fell ill?
>
> HH: Yes, my eyesight on the left is bad; and I can't read as well as I used to.
>
> E: How would you describe your reading problem?
>
> HH: It is just slower than before and more stressful. Sometimes I omit words at the beginning of a line. Often I realize it only when I get to the end of a sentence and it does not make sense. Sometimes when I get to the end of a line I can't find the beginning of the next. Or I skip a whole line.
>
> E: Have you any other problems with your vision?
>
> HH: Yes, sometimes I don't notice people on the left till too late, and then I bump into them.
>
> E: What's your sense of direction like when you go out?
>
> HH: It's bad, and when there's a lot going on it takes a lot longer for me to find things, especially when they are on the left.

Now compare this with a patient suffering from an attentional disturbance: Neglect (N). Answering the same questions.

>E: Have you noticed any changes in your vision since you fell ill [right middle cerebral artery infarction]?
>
>N: No, none that I know of. Except – there's something not quite right with my glasses.
>
>E: Do you have problems with reading?
>
>N: No, not really.
>
>E: Do you sometimes miss words on one side of the page when you are reading?
>
>N: No, I've never noticed that.
>
>E: Have you noticed that your vision is not so good on one side, for example on the left?
>
>N: My left eye is fine.
>
>E: Do you sometimes bump into things on one side or overlook people on one side more often than you used to?
>
>N: Well, sometimes I bump into things, true. But that is only because there's such a lot of "people out and about – and people are so inconsiderate."
>
>E: What's your sense of direction like when you go out?
>
>N: I find everything that I want to find.

Not only is there a huge deficit, but the awareness of it has also completely disappeared as well. Another reaction also illustrates this. This patient is suffering from 'neglect' and is missing an important function of the right hemisphere: our connection to reality.

> *"I knew the word 'neglect' was a sort of medical term for whatever was wrong, but the word bothered me, because you only neglect something that is actually there, don't you? If it is not there, how can you neglect it? It does not seem right to me that the word 'neglect' should be used to describe it. I think they thought I was definitely, deliberately not looking to the left. I wasn't really ... If it is not there you're not neglecting it"*

Another example is a test in which a person has to choose if a red or blue light will turn on. After a while it becomes clear the red light blinks 66% of the time while the blue one blinks 33% of the time. A brain with a problem in the right hemisphere and thus a dominant left hemisphere will gamble 66% red and 33 % blue, because it's logical. A person with a problem in the left hemisphere and thus a dominant right hemisphere will choose red 100% of the time, because it's rational. Because red has always the highest probability of blinking.

Or try this one. Read the following statement:
"The desert is full of snow and ice, it's very cold."

Patients who have a problem in the right hemisphere will think this is both correct and logical, because it has an internal logic. A properly functioning right hemisphere, our bullshit detector, tells us what it is: bullshit.

Or an ethical test. Which one is worse? A person thinks he puts poison in someone's tea to kill a person, but actually puts in sugar and the person lives. Or a person who thinks it puts sugar in someone's tea, but actually puts in poison and the person dies? Somebody with an artificially reduced right hemisphere will say the person who killed somebody is worse, because our left hemisphere has a way to prioritize causal relations (like a machine). Someone is dead, who did it, the person who puts poison in the tea. People with a functioning right hemisphere are more likely to think the intention is more important than the result. Our right hemisphere holds our humanity. Our left hemisphere is a great emissary but a terrible master.

An interesting observation Iain McGilchrist makes is that patients who see things that are not there, almost always have a problem in their right hemisphere. So he suspects that plant medicines, or nature-based hallucinogens, actually suppress the right hemisphere and don't liberate it, as it is often discussed. But he doesn't make a decisive statement about it, as he did with the other statements that are in the table.

Without a properly functioning left hemisphere we are prone to depression (too much reality). Most people with autism and schizophrenia have problems with their right hemisphere (too little connection with reality). McGilchrist compares the modern world with a mild case of schizophrenia. We collectively believe we're making progress but we are actually destroying our own reality. McGilchrist: "We live in our own bubble, confabulating (making up stories) when asked the simplest question on why we do things. Being more focused on brands and images than on the material, concrete and natural world."

McGilchrist also concludes we now live in a culture that increasingly focuses on the information presented by our left hemisphere. But it's also clear that this causes our greatest problems. It results in us living our lives as if reality is secondary and our representations are primary.

The reason is unclear, but it's a fact that our brain hemispheres have grown bigger the past decades while the connection between the two hemispheres has weakend. This means that our brain is making it harder to get out of our hypnotizing, over-confident, confabulating left hemisphere. The left doesn't want to be bothered by reality. In order to counter this, we can make a conscious choice to request information from the right hemisphere. This would create a healthy balance. Dance, poetry, humor, art, food, the material world. Without their concepts, labels, abstractions, or philosophical chatter. Just as they are.

Like Taleb, McGilchrist has to invent words to describe something they experience in reality. Like our culture, our language has drifted away from what is real. For Taleb it is antifragile. For listening to our right hemisphere McGilchrist uses the word *presencing:* "Anything that strikes you of immediate importance. When there is no preexisting story of what is going to happen next. It is what we stop doing when we get older, but poetry can reignite in us." It is what happens when we embrace the unknown.

The two hemispheres also have very different perspectives on what is objective. Objectivity for the left hemisphere means the world is out there and we are in here, trying to be as correct as possible about what is out there, which is viewed as a fixed thing. Our left hemisphere is obsessed with being certain about things and it separates us from what we're looking at. Quantum mechanics and social science has shown us that this is a wrong idea about reality. We are not separate from anything that we observe. Seeing something objectively is impossible from the idea that it is 'out there'.

This idea about objectivity makes it very likely to fall for the trap to look for progress in things that can be measured. While most things that have value can't be measured.

Objectivity for the right hemisphere starts with knowing it can only know reality within the limitations of our own brain. The right hemisphere knows what it doesn't know. The right hemisphere also knows it is part of reality, the observer and the thing it is looking at are creating each other and are inseparable.

McGilchrist: "Our right hemisphere views objectivity as a

take on reality that is an ever evolving belief acquired through imagining as many possible perspectives as possible." Objectivity as a process, reality as a flow. Where objectivity is measured not in correctness but by experience. I love it.

Science for the left hemisphere is a protocol based, bureaucratic, dead thing. Looking for ways to manipulate the world and excluding information from our right hemisphere.

Science for the right hemisphere is a humble approach to get closer to reality, which is an alive process, full of imagination, intuition and reason that includes information from the left hemisphere.

In our time of transformation not only our idea of a solution is going to change. Our whole understanding of what reality is made of is changing. Reality is not just a thing, it is a movement, where everything is influencing everything all the time. Are you ready for it?

A good indicator that we need a new paradigm is when the old paradigm fails to identify and improve the most important matters at hand. The past seventy years have shown us clearly that we have a great problem doing that. Our reality is drastically changing and if we don't act accordingly we will destroy our own reality. The old paradigm, the paradigm of things, the paradigm where we are separate from reality is a helpful metaphor for a part of reality. The model of the world as a movement, and a process, in which we are an inseparable part of it, is better.

To summarize, we ground ourselves into what is real by presencing the world. To sense the world before we give it labels. Experiencing live without a pre-existing story. Sounds like listening to the river below the river, as Clarissa Pinkola Estes calls it. Or following the signs of the road as Pablo Caelo calls it. Letting the information from your presencing capacities lead your life means Embodying Reality. Not a new story about how things should be (another abstraction), but an embodiment of what is real and important.

Into the unknown

Reconnecting with reality feels like falling to me. You fall into something and often it's a complete shock and surprise. It helps not going out and looking for it, but just letting it happen. Like falling asleep or falling in love. Trying to manipulate it only activates the problem even more. We reconnect with reality by opening up and letting it happen.

> *"The bad news is you're falling through the air.*
> *Nothing to hang on to, no parachute.*
> *The good news is there's no ground."*
> Chögyam Trungpa Rinpoche, Buddhist meditation master

What sustainability needs is a new dominant paradigm for all of humanity. Designing this paradigm for other people is exactly what got us into this mess. It means we continue to colonize the world while being increasingly sure that we're doing good.

What the new paradigm needs is to reconnect with reality. This way a new story will emerge naturally, one that will continue to flow and unfold through time.

This doesn't happen if we focus our attention on new technologies, legislation, solutions or stories. That's just more left brain hemisphere taking the lead. We need the right hemisphere to be our guide and reconnect us with what is real. Designing a new paradigm is not going to improve anything. We need to trust life and honor what emerges. True sustainability means to enter an entirely new world. We need to open our state of being to the world, fall into reality once again and learn to trust the miracle of life.

Thankfully, this is a familiar path. It's where almost every story we know begins. Whether it's Neo, Harry, Frodo, Alice or Buddha. Their story begins with entering an unknown world. Breaking free from their familiar myth and going back into the wilderness, the wilderness being a metaphor for the unknown. As Joseph Campbell clearly points out in his book, *The Hero With a Thousand Faces*.

The journey through the unknown is a wild path. We let go of our familiar myth and experience reality without our old filter getting in the way.

The modern myth doesn't make it very easy on us to break out and experience reality without this old filter. Which is always the case with a dominant myth. If a myth doesn't reject the wild path, it's difficult to become the dominant myth. The wild path is the opposite of following a shared story.

As with our myth, we have mostly lost the language for this wild path. Just to start somewhere: the modern myth often describes reality as something for barbaric or reckless people. To seek unnecessary risk is reckless and to cause unnecessary harm is barbaric. The wild path is something else, something global crises are teaching us all over again. You can step into an unknown world, prepare well, make informed choices, and still stay open to see beyond your own perspective and expectations. The wild path is more of an attitude than an action, and it doesn't have to mean walking away from the place you live.

Wild paths are completely personal journeys because the unknown presents itself as something different for each one of us. Working on a myth is also a very intimate issue because everyone has experienced different conditioning in their past.

There is no need to go look for a wild path. Daily life pulls you out of your own ideas of what is normal often enough. What helps is just to be open to it, allow it to come and try to avoid immediately seeking out what is familiar, when things start to get uncomfortable.

Sometimes the wild path is a conscious choice, but most of the time it just happens. Sometimes it comes from inspiration, but mostly it's a necessity, a crisis, that pulls us out of what is familiar and makes us crash into reality.

Letting go of what is known is not as easy as it sounds. You can literally travel the world and come home with the same myth you left with, and be overjoyed about your successful journey. You can also come home with a new myth after just one unexpected encounter with a stranger on your own street.

On a wild path, we wake up from our myth's hypnosis and learn to reconnect with reality. And by doing so, we learn to see what's natural and enhances the whole, and what's a myth detached from reality and makes the world increasingly turbulent.

Not entirely coincidentally, the Brothers Grimm's folk tale "Iron John" also begins with going into the unknown. It's the folk tale Robert Bly uses in his book to describe men's initiations into mature masculinity, which I've already mentioned. The first chapter of Bly's *Iron John* explains this by using symbolism. It goes something like this:

> *A long time ago an adventurer entered a new kingdom. When he arrived at the capital, the adventurer walked up to the castle and asked for an audience with the king. "Is there anything dangerous to do here?", the adventurer asked the king. After a moment of thought, the king replies: "No, everything is safe here. We're good."*
>
> *He was silent for a moment.*
>
> *"Come to think of it, there is a place in the Forbidden Forest that no one comes back from. But I guess that's not what you mean."*
>
> *"That's exactly the sort of thing I mean", said the adventurer and together with his dog, his best friend and only companion, he sets off to the Forbidden Forest in search of the place no one comes back from.*
>
> *After a long walk through the forest, the trees give way and the adventurer sees a clearing with a pond in the*

middle. His dog runs ahead and when he's near the water, a giant hand comes out of the pond and grabs the dog and pulls him under the water.

The adventurer thinks: "This must be the place", and he returns to the castle to round up more men and some buckets.

With their help, the adventurer begins to empty the pond. After a long time, when the pond is nearly empty, they find a large hairy man at the bottom. His body is covered with a sort of orange-brown hair, like the color of rusty iron. The wild man is unconscious. The adventurer picks up the wild man and carries him back to the city.

We can view the adventurer as a symbol for anyone who is curious about the world beyond our shared myth and is brave enough to take the wild path. The adventurer is clearly on a journey into an unknown world. When we're on the wild path, we see the world as it is because that's what the wilderness does to you. Anything can happen, so we are on constant alert. We are completely present in the current moment. The wild path is not a wild path if it doesn't take courage to embark on it. As scary as the wilderness is, if you don't feel that fear, you don't have your attention focused on what's real either. Then, you still operate based on a story that everything is supposedly safe, and that gets in your way. When we see the world as it is once again, we see the beauty of the world, as well as its dangers and uncertainties.

The romance of adventure in stories is largely exaggerated. The world beyond the familiar myth is unimaginably beautiful and incredibly ugly at the same time. We see beautiful nature, but also the cruelty of nature. We see our talent, but also our shadow. In a healthy forest, living and dead trees can be seen side by side.

You cannot see reality selectively. You either see all the beauty and all the ugliness, or you only see the confirmation of your own myth. That's why when you examine climate change, for instance, you also encounter poverty, racism, and the mass extinction of plant and animal species. But you also encounter the beauty of nature, the existing old-growth forests, the communities that care for the wilderness, and the indigenous wisdom that still lives on.

In the fairy tale, the adventurer loses his most loyal and dear friend, his dog. If we don't shy away from that trauma, but stick to it and do our work, we will encounter a wild person at the bottom of the pond.

'Doing our work' stands for peeling off our personality, layer by layer. Being open to the world as it is, is also about letting go of the myth we trust about ourselves. Our self-image is full of truths and myths. Exploring our personality is hard work. In the story, the buckets and the emptying of the pond symbolize this. We can also be so frightened by the trauma, or the hard work, that we run back to the city and never go back into the wilderness again. If we do this, we'd rather accept the 'normal' suffering experienced in the city than take a chance on the potential of a new opportunity.

A wild path in our daily life could be, for example, giving a presentation. There is little that frightens us as much as receiving the group's full attention. The anxiety of the moment allows us to let the world show itself as it is. It brings us into a heightened state of awareness, as every performance can do. While we can learn the most from receiving the group's full attention, it's also the place we avoid the most. The modern myth has us terrified of 'what's out there', while we plunder it and, by doing so, threaten our own safety.

When we do our work and meet the wild man at the bottom of our psyche for the first time, we are so incredibly amazed we want to show him off to others. The adventurer brings the unconscious wild man back to town, just as we do when we return from a journey, a retreat, or find a new love. When we have made a new discovery outside of our known story, we immediately share it with our loved ones to make it part of our myth as quickly as possible.

The wilderness in ourselves, the wild man, is unconscious. Modern people are unaware of their own wild nature. They have their story of life at heart and think their life is going well to the extent that their life meets their expectations.

At the castle, news of the adventurer and the wild man has already reached the king before the adventurer gets there. The wild man is quickly chained up and put in an iron cage and the town buzzes with stories of all the terrible things the wild man has done. The king has the cage set up in the middle of the square, where everyone can see him.

Standing next to the cage, the king delivers a thunderous sermon.

The wild man is "the greatest danger to our way of life" and "any contact with the wild man is forbidden." On the king's command, anyone who helps him escape will be killed immediately. At the end of his sermon, he gives the key to the cage to the queen for safe keeping. Anxiously, the townspeople stay far away from the cage that holds the dangerous wild man.

Days go by, until one morning something unexpected happens.

The king's son is playing in the castle's gallery with his favorite golden ball. Until he accidentally loses the ball, and it rolls down the stairs, bounces over the floor, into the cage and comes to a stop in front of the hairy legs of the wild man.

The boy walks to the cage and, in a trembling voice, asks the wild man if he can have his golden ball back.

> "You'll get your golden ball back", the wild man replies, "if you'll strip me of these chains and free me from the cage".
> The boy stammers, "But... I don't know where the key is".
> "The key is under the pillow of the queen", says the wild man.
> The boy has an idea and sneaks into his parents' bedroom unseen. He feels under his mother's pillow and his fingers snatch the keys from under it.

The adventurer underestimated the city's reaction, and the discovery of the wild man is not investigated or celebrated, but the wild man is chained and caged. The city symbolizes the dominant idea of what is "normal" in society. Anything that does not belong to this dominant idea is loathed and separated from the rest. In the city, we are made to fear the unknown.

In the city, there is a story for everything: 'this is how' you eat, 'this is how' you do school, 'this is how' you do work, 'this is how' families work and 'this is how' you hang out with friends. The only accepted way of living well in the city is to follow these stories as closely as possible. That is, excelling at being normal. People in the city trust their stories about the world and are no longer curious about the stories of the wild man, or the adventurer. The cage is a symbol for this. We prefer to experience the world through the language of our loved ones, rather than explore it on our own. So we immediately believe that the wild man is dangerous, and it's better to stay away from him.

The king's son plays with his golden ball which, like in the tale "The Princess and the Frog", symbolizes his natural talent. Children are still connected with their natural talent and, to them, it feels like the most common thing in the world.

Talent is that which we do naturally. Our talent is what we can't help but do. It's so natural to us that we easily overlook it. Then we lose our talent and discover it once again, when we learn to see ourselves from outside of our stories. Then we notice again what we do naturally and that's our talent. Learning to listen to the 'river below the river' is also a skill for discovering our talent, and discovering when we are in our element. It's a way of learning to focus on what is real.

At some point during our childhood, we lose touch with our natural talent and it comes into possession of the wild man residing in each one of us. Because our loved ones tell stories of the horrors of the wild man, most people don't dare reach out to the wild man to ask for their golden ball. The boy's greatest sign of courage is his choice to do so. It's the moment the boy steps outside the city's familiar stories and begins his journey on his own wild path. The great escape. Like the original story of "The Princess and the Frog", we find our place in the world by breaking the rules, not by following them. If we follow the rules, we find success in the eyes of others. If we step out of our familiar stories, we find our own success.

The adventurer found the wild man by not running away from trauma (losing his loyal friend). The boy finds contact with the wild man by not running away from what's happening in his everyday life. The boy misses his golden ball, just like most of us miss meaningful work, time with our loved ones, intimacy, and using our own talent. Strangely enough, we think we will find these things by working harder on our plans and goals, and we end up adding even more stories through training and reading books. Which puts us more and more in a "motivation from cognitive construct" mode of being, which is the domain of the left hemisphere. The opposite is what's true: We find them when we let go of our known myth and focus on what is real.

Here we encounter a problem just as we do when working on our myth. Going into the wilderness doesn't necessarily mean quitting your job, breaking up your relationship, or traveling the world. If you enter the wild path with the expectation that it's a wild path, then it's not free of expectations and stories. Maybe staying in a not-so-great job is the unknown for you and that which brings you to a new richness in life. Or maybe starting a family is the unknown for you and not starting your own business. So wild paths are very personal endeavors, just like working on a myth. And just like a myth, you don't get there through thinking, language, lists, plans, control or willpower. It's the very act of letting go of all those things that makes something a wild path.

So it doesn't help you to go looking for a wild path, because then you're in the realm of expectations. Falling into reality happens when we see our imagined reality for what it is: a myth.

It's noteworthy that, from this point on, the adventurer does not appear in the story of *Iron John*. In the West, there is a culture of masculinity in which "the hero" is labeled as a mature form. Someone who wins, overcomes the challenge and goes where no one else dares. The fact that this is seen as mature is a mistake. The hero and the adventurer symbolize the developed boy. They do everything for the thrill, the story and to win. Mature people go beyond these things. The adventurer goes from one plan to another and is not necessarily in the service of something greater. The adventurer knows the wild man, but does not learn from him.

So the adventurer, the eternal child, goes back to looking for his next adventure, but the king's son wants his natural talent back. To get his ball back, he must outwit his parents. The king and queen symbolize the dominant myth of the city, as does the castle and everyone who works in it. These are the people who best live up to the myth of the city. The people with social status and success. To find his talent again, he must let go of that story, going beyond that idea of success and progress, as well as beyond the false security of the palace and the social status that the king's son has in that world.

The location of the key to open the cage is under the queen's pillow, which symbolizes the mother's dreams of her ideal son.

If the son stays in the city, he may become a respected knight, blacksmith, or doctor. Exactly what his mother envisioned. His natural talent and job satisfaction will not be fulfilled in this way, and this also applies to us. We discover these qualities through the wild man and not by obediently following the myths of our environment. Mothers get in the way with all their well-intentioned expectations and, due to our love for our mothers, this also makes them stand in our way. Until we want our golden ball back and do so by freeing our inner wild man.

The son could also ask or demand the key back from the queen, but then he will stay within his mother's expectations. Stealing the key is essential. This is how we learn to experience reality of which our myth is just a part. In which the mother's loving intentions get in the way. Love coming from a shared myth is nothing more than good intentions.

> *Full of adrenaline, the boy sprints back to the cage, opens it and frees the wild man from his chains. The guards see the open cage of the wild man and sound the alarm. "Quick, follow me!", says the boy. The boy leads the wild man through a secret passage, through the gate and outside the city walls. Meanwhile, the whole town is in an uproar and the boy realizes what he has done. "Oh no, they're going to kill me."*
>
> *"Then you better come with me", says the wild man.*

> "I have a house in the forest with riches so great they are beyond your imagination. Just climb on my shoulders".
> The boy climbs on the wild man's shoulders and together they walk into the wilderness. And then the wild man says, "My name is Iron John. What's yours?"

By going into the wilderness with Iron John, the boy gets away from the familiar myth. He throws away his father's book of rules by not following the rules of the city, but going with Iron John. Our father gives us a manual on how we are supposed to handle life. This is important to be able to participate in the power of humans. Only the world outside of our myth remains beyond our reach. The father can also be read as society as a whole: education, religion, or work, also give us a book of rules. Following a book of rules is something with which we can collect plenty of status and money, but if we do so, the miracle of life will stay out of our reach.

Giving children the space to discover reality for themselves is a crucial part of parenting. It's important for the child, but also for the people in the city. It allows the child to reveal the blind spots of the older generations, which need to start supporting the new generation instead of colonizing it. The young have a better view of the blind spots, but are missing the experiences and resources that the older generations have in order to make something from it.

The wealth of the wild man in the woods is a richness that

people in the city can no longer imagine. This wealth is actually about doing soulful work, being one with nature, communicating with the universal intelligence, true friendship, love-making that lasts the night. Qualities we do not find in the world of stories. The wealth of the forest is the wealth of the right column from the tables we saw previously, all of which can be found outside of the systems we trust and inside of ourselves. It's the miracle of life.

If we don't throw away the book of rules and steal the key from under the pillow, then we use the insight of a myth to optimize our lives. If we don't fall into reality, then we continue to look for social status and success the way the modern myth does. To get out of that, the wild path is essential. Otherwise we just continue to do our best to follow or design "the good myth."

The modern myth's first trick to avoid looking past our learned perceptions is the belief that there is no myth and that ideas about love, social status, success and progress are fixed and known. Its second trick is that we tend to imagine what a wild path should look like. Such as, going wild can be starting your own business, jumping out of a helicopter or dancing on a bar. As soon as we begin a story, we're already creating expectations and not presencing what is. If we make the wild path part of the known story, it's no longer wild but tamed. The wild is precisely everything that is not tamed. A wild path is being in the moment and feeling connected to reality.

The cage that the king puts the wild man in has two meanings. The first is to represent the city's fear of the unknown. The king uses that fear to maintain the shared myth and secure both order and power. The second meaning is to reveal the fact that we ourselves cage the wild man when we come back to the city after walking the wild path, just as the adventurer does. We tell stories of our discoveries and experiences on the wild path, forgetting what got us there: experiencing what is when we let go of the familiar stories.

When people are touched by the ecological decay and social injustice they see in reality, they quickly write stories, concepts and theories about it. Then try to convince as many people as possible of their story. This is how they put Iron John back in a cage. The same thing goes for people who come back from a retreat or a trail, they use their increased connection with the miracle of life to improve their separate systems. Therefore, the systems they trust are still leading their lives.

For the people in the city, the story of sustainability is a story that is added to their lives, which therefore become more and more complicated. What the city people need is not a new story, but the courage to ask Iron John for their golden ball, step through the gate into the unknown and fall into reality. Every day anew.

"A Zen master once lived high in the mountains, where a son of a wealthy family was sent to learn about Zen. After a long and impatient journey, the son arrived at the house of the Zen master. Who greeted him warmly, welcomed him and let him stay in his house.

They ate together, walked together, drank tea together, and the days passed slowly. Until the student asks, "Master, when do the classes begin?"

"What do you mean?" replies the master, "classes have long since begun."

The son looks at him in bewilderment, "but we haven't done anything yet?"

"Have I not welcomed you into my home, thanked you when you poured tea for me, listened to you when you said something, and walked beside you when we went out? I don't have a better explanation of the essence of life for you."

DT Suzuki, *Essays on Zen* (1961)

Part III
Falling into reality

Guiding without steering

The hypnosis of our myth is so strong that it can be confusing if we're dealing with reality or with our imagined reality. A country, technology, legislation, and money are clear things, but our thoughts, feelings and motivations are more complex. Some are real, others we make real. We learn about ourselves and grow our self-knowledge when we step into the unknown and presence the world again with our right hemisphere capabilities.

On a wild path, you have to do the work yourself, but thankfully you don't have to do it alone. There are also guides. People who guide you on your wild path without filling your space with their story. Wayfinders, I call them. The king's son in the folk tale is not alone either, Iron John is his wayfinder.

People who help us to stay on our path and don't push us into a new myth, these are the kind of guides we need. Wayfinders guide you without expecting anything from you. Wayfinders are as scarce as real friends and, in my experience, they become both pretty quickly. In true friendship, we find love without having to conform to any myth. You can be yourself with them. Completely.

You can't encourage someone to fall into reality and go on a wild path, because then that someone is fulfilling your expectations and there's still a myth in the way. The best you can do is to be present with someone, without wanting anything other than what is there. That's loving without creating a story about love.

That's what wise teachers, parents, managers and friends have in common. Being present and not trying to add anything. The only thing they help with is preventing you from becoming unnecessarily reckless or barbaric. Wayfinders know how to do that.

I have been fortunate to have met a number of wayfinders. They are people who have reached the maturity that Bly and Estés describe. They have discovered life's hidden treasures, made them their own, and now guide others on their path to their hidden treasures. Wayfinders have both feet in the systems we trust and both feet in reality. They move effortlessly between the two and remain very casual about it.

For me, they're proof you can live fully and respond realistically to global crises at the same time. They know how to Embody Reality, make the two worlds work together and they also know how to help people reconnect with reality.

Every conversation with them feels like a wild path. After every interaction, I go back home with a grounded myth. Everything that happens with them becomes an intense experience that lays a foundation for a new myth.

Although the people who have become my wayfinders do very different things, they have much in common. For starters, they are all over seventy years old. My inspiration for our response to global crises comes from people who are rich in life's experiences. Good wayfinders can usually be recognized by their reverence for their own wayfinders. No one reaches maturity without help.

No one completely becomes free of their myth's hypnosis on their own. We need real friends.

The wayfinders I have learned from have all found their own craft and a way to be autonomous in their craft within the current system. They have also sought the root of their craft: the wayfinders of my wayfinders are indigenous people from all over the world.

My wayfinders all exude tremendous calm and yet are full of vigor in the world. They remain relaxed and alert at the same time, even when they're under pressure. They've found a way to maintain a constant calm in the midst of turbulence without denying or ignoring global crises. They also clearly admit what they don't know, and yet they act confidently in the world.

They show you that all events in life can be part of a journey towards more connection to the miracle of life. Enjoying more and more, giving more and more, being more and more of a wayfinder for others, giving and receiving more and more insights, and being more and more present. Retirement is a concept they do not adhere to. They're all still working at their own pace.

What they also have in common is the depth of a simple life. On the outside they lead a simple life, but once you speak to them you find clear depth. Their life and success are separate from materialism. Their dignity is separate from status symbols in society. They enjoy giving their talent to the world and that's enough. They're very casual about that. Their talent looks like the most common thing in the world, yet it's world-class and it takes decades to master it up to their level.

I have never been able to catch them setting a condition for a good life. They know the best ancient rituals, techniques, methods and language, but they will never say you must know them for a good life. If you want to learn from them and they accept you as a student, they will share with you whatever they feel is appropriate for you at that time. You don't have to do anything for them, but if you want to learn from them, then certain things have to be done.

Meditating, taking a cold shower, doing yoga every morning and eating vegan food are all fine rituals if they fit your path. But to take a step too far and say that a good life only comes when you do these things is to put yet another myth at center stage.

People who set conditions for a good life are mainly concerned with binding followers to them, and less concerned with expressing what their myth stands for. Having to be able to maintain a certain yoga posture, sing a song flawlessly, sit still for two hours, give away all your money, or feel a certain chakra are all examples of how a myth is put at the center. Wayfinders know that it doesn't take much to fall into reality and step into the miracle of life. It's not a process, but a realization after which something is set in motion. If you can't do that without help, then they can guide you in that. Although they will never make any promises. They can't do it for you and they don't control what happens in life either.

For instance, Iron John only helps the boy when the young

prince asks for it. Robert Bly adapted the original story of "Iron John" in the Brothers Grimm anthology. The story in the volume is only a shadow of the story Robert Bly made of it. What they have in common is that Iron John is always there for the boy in the woods. When the boy walks to the woods and calls Iron John three times, the boy's wayfinder is there for him. The initiative to learn remains with the young prince. Therefore, the young prince continues to experience reality and doesn't fall into the trap of experiencing the world through the perspective of his guide.

My wayfinders all encourage me to learn from other teachers as well. They ask only for the necessary money. I come when I have a question and when I want to learn something. Beyond that, they let me be. Wayfinders are completely interested and completely detached at the same time. They are also my best examples of a good learner. Without hesitation, they step into a learning mode and become the student once again when it's appropriate.

The wayfinders I know prefer not to talk about the myth. They treat it like a secret. When I tell them I'm writing a book about the myth as a path to a realistic response to global crises, I usually get only a meaningful smile and sometimes something like: "Nice challenge you've taken on." They know the myth, work on grounding myths as best as they can, and yet they don't talk about it. I think it's because they don't want to cage Iron John.

> *"Those who know,*
> *don't talk about it.*
> *Those who talk about it,*
> *don't know."*
>
> Lao Tzu, Dao de Jing (about 500 BC)

The main effect they have on me is that my trust in life grows. They don't give me an increasingly clever story on how to deal with life, but with them my trust in what happens grows. This makes letting go of old stories that no longer work for me easier. It's also less confronting to look at my own shadow, trauma, or inhibiting beliefs. This is because there is also something bigger than my myth and I can trust that too. My myth becomes more open and it becomes a little easier to keep it connected to the moment and the world as it is. This is exactly what one needs in order to detach from having 'our ego at the center of everything'. Falling into reality, taking the wild path and getting better and better at acting from reality instead of reacting from our known myth is what we think we need to do. Moving from a life for love to a life from love.

    Finding a wayfinder for yourself is like falling in love. It just happens, but doing nothing doesn't help either. What does help is doing what you genuinely enjoy, and asking for help for something you want to learn or overcome. Start prioritizing something real, wayfinders notice this immediately. Because they know how hard it is. If you find one, stay critical and open. Wayfinders form you for life and many people are far too eager to be a guide, so they fail to see that they are pushing you in their myth. Helping people by adding a myth does not bring people closer to reality.

When looking for a guide, it helps to ask yourself: Are they themselves the best example of their own message? Do they set conditions for a good life? Do they limit my free will in any way? Do they listen to my unique situation? Can I become just as good as them in less than forty years? If the answer is yes, then there are probably better ones out there.

Of course, we shouldn't overdo it. Sometimes you discover what suits you best by going with what is. Also, you don't have to ask anyone for confirmation if someone is a wayfinder for you, you just know. Just like falling in love.

When we fall into reality we rediscover reality. We find it's quite different from what we assume it is. It's not a collection of things, it's not a machine, it's not something we can exploit without it affecting ourselves, there is no self-interest in reality. The way to go about it isn't to be smart, save some money, work hard, set goals, plan ahead, save for retirement and be nice to people. Words that fit better are surrender, not knowing, intention, grounding, and connection.

Wayfinders know this and show us how to Embody Reality and guide others in reconnecting with reality as well. I'll share my experiences with five wayfinders and their ways to reconnect with reality in the next five chapters. But, for starters, I think this verse from the *Dao de Jing* sums it up perfectly.

> *"Those in ancient times who acted according to the Dao,*
> *were subtle, mysterious, dark, penetrating.*
> *So inscrutable that they could not be known.*
> *Therefore I make an attempt to describe their outward appearance.*
>
> *Cautious, as if crossing a river in winter.*
> *Vigilant, as if they have neighbors to fear on four sides.*
> *Reserved, like a guest.*
> *Dissolved, like melting ice.*
> *Unspoiled, like untreated wood.*
> *Vast, like a valley.*
> *Undifferentiated, like muddy water."*
>
> Lao Tzu, Dao de Jing (500 BC)

A field of energy

In Amsterdam I found a wayfinder in Sensei Jan Kallenbach who teaches Tai Ki Kenpo in his Shin-Shinbuken dojo. Sensei was one of the first westerners allowed to train with the masters in Japan. The teacher who became his lifelong example was Kenichi Sawai.

Sawai Sensei founded the martial art of Tai Ki Kenpo in the 1940s. Kenichi Sawai was a Budo master in Japan and mastered numerous styles. He did what no Japanese did in his time, which was to learn Chinese styles. He traveled to China and found in Wang Chang Chai his teacher in the martial art of Yi Chuan and, for the next three years, trained with him. The combination of his Japanese experience and the insights he learned in China grew into the martial art of Tai Ki Kenpo.

To understand the idea behind these martial arts, it's helpful if we understand their names. Yi stands for 'intention', where head and heart come together. Chuan stands for 'work' and 'mastery'. It's classical Chinese boxing focusing the power of your mind and intention as the source of your strength.

Tai means both 'work' and 'mastery' in Japanese. Ki stands for 'life energy'. Kenpo stands for 'fist art'. The combined Chinese and Japanese influences make the movements in Tai Ki Kenpo look round, fluid, explosive and powerful, all at the same time. Like poetry in movement. It's a fusion of the strict and minimalist Japanese Budo with the circular and mystical movements from the Chinese arts.

My Sensei, Jan Kallenbach, has become a phenomenon in both the Dutch and international martial arts world. He is the first Dutchman to become European Champion in an Eastern martial art, in Kyokushin Karate in 1974. He started in Judo, grew in karate and found his master in Sawai Sensei and Tai Ki Kenpo in Japan.

Jan was a Physical Education college teacher and saved enough each year to travel to Japan during his summer vacations and train there for two months. Twice he traveled for two weeks on the Trans-Siberian Express to make this possible. He's my example of being sincere in what you want to learn. Jan Kallenbach is my wayfinder. His wayfinder is Sawai. Sawai's wayfinder is Master Wang Chang Chai and so on. Learning from a wayfinder usually means you step into a lineage, a tradition.

Tai Ki Kenpo is all about learning to move freely. Learning to read the opponent so well that you are faster. Learning to feel so well that your body knows where there is a gap in the opponent's defenses. Everything is focused on beating the opponent by moving freely. There are no competitions, belts or other structures to be found in Tai Ki Kenpo. Fighting and free movement do not fit into categories, labels and rules. All levels train together and the Sensei indicates whether you are junior, senior, or teacher level. That's it. It's an art for a lifetime. If you do your best, you will start to understand Tai Ki after ten years of training. You will be able to practice it properly after twenty years, and after thirty years, you will be able to teach others. No guarantees are given about how many years it can take you though.

The most important and most difficult exercise we do is standing still. Every class starts with half an hour of Ritsu Zen, or Standing Zen. No explanations are given, you just copy the other people present. You learn to fall into reality at Tai Ki Kenpo through the dynamics of standing still.

After half an hour of Ritsu Zen, there are some techniques that we practice with each other. They're always focused on learning to move freely. Technique is subservient to spontaneity. Which means learning to relax a lot, even when you're put under stress. Somebody tries to hit you and somehow the reflex of most people is to stop breathing. Our conditioning in the modern world is to be unaware of the reality of our own body. Especially when we're experiencing stress.

The power of Tai Ki comes from Ki. The life energy that comes along with the movements you do through your intention. This also allows you to defeat opponents that are stronger and heavier than yourself. Sawai Sensei showed us that it's the smartest fighter who wins, not necessarily the biggest. Sawai was small and a featherweight, but at the first meeting with my sensei, he easily defeated the heavyweight giant from Amsterdam.

Fighting is an excellent way to fall into reality and be in the moment. You become aware of your tense muscles and restrained breathing. It takes training to stay with your natural-relaxed-alert self. While training in Tai Ki, people rarely talk about the philosophy of what we are doing. Everybody is focused on doing the exercises and helping each other grow. As soon as you start talking about it, the Sensei says, "Show me." The focus is on reality, your story about it is secondary.

In the dojo, the people who train the longest are the best. No matter how old they are. I've been training there for ten years, but I can't match the speed and strength of the much older men who have been training there for over 40 years. Yet everyone treats each other with the same respect. The hierarchy on the mat says nothing about the manners outside of the mat. This, once again, shows that mental development is central at Tai Ki Kenpo. The whole person grows from moving with intention.

Finding compassion in someone who tries to hit your face is a fascinating discovery. Everyone is growing with each other by responding appropriately. If you're better than your opponent, you can let the other person feel that without unnecessarily hurting them. The fact that no one crosses a line is essential for this. That's the challenge for people with more experience who train with people with less experience. In the dojo, men learn to feel limits without talking. If you are too careful, then you get hit. If you are too hard, then no one learns. Thankfully, the Sensei sees everything. That's not a myth. He really sees everything.

The effect of training in the dojo is a miracle by itself. On the bicycle to the dojo my head is full, my feelings are racing in all directions and my concentration is all over the place. After the lesson, I feel peace, clarity and a sense of fullness. Something transforms by being engaged in fighting from this place of stillness. Something I only partially get from running, kickboxing or crossfit. Learning to fight has become the main cornerstone for my mental health and spiritual development.

It's so consistent, such a sharp difference between before and after, and after ten years I still don't know exactly how that happened or when it happened. Something is working while we're at it. Helping each other train is a more important goal than hurting one another. Although, good training usually means really trying to hit the other person, otherwise it doesn't work. Usually, at the first touch, you know which of the two is better. If you're not sure about it, you know it's going to be interesting.

The structure of the lesson is minimal. There are more principles than there are structures to adhere to. Everyone moves differently, everyone gets different feedback and different focus points. Yet, it's still recognizably Tai Ki Kenpo and, after ten years, I still cannot describe why it's recognizably the same source of moving. How the Sensei does this fascinates me, and it works consistently with everyone who trains regularly.

In this martial art, there is full attention, concentration, flow, a human-centered approach and a sense of unity. The more you are one while fighting, the better you can read someone's moves. It's about becoming good at fighting by becoming one with the opponent. Unity as a way of winning, which is not just about overpowering the opponent. Winning is doing what is appropriate in the situation.

In meditation, or being alone in nature for a long time, I could experience a more subtle field than what meets the eye. Through Tai Ki Kenpo I learned to work on this on a weekly basis. To feel both the power and strength when mind, body and heart are aligned and to be reminded of the miracle of life. The core exercise for this, that has been passed on for millennia by warriors in the East and finally found its way to my sensei and his dojo in Amsterdam, is standing still.

It looks like a QiGong pose and what it does is nothing short of magic. In the beginning, it sharpens the mind for what is happening in the body. Later, it also makes you aware of the subtle energy that moves through and around your body. Up to the point where you can maintain this meditative state while moving and even fighting. In this way, fighting becomes a healing experience. The Japanese name for this is Budo. Bu means 'fighting skills'. Do means 'spiritual path'. My sensei's life is about keeping Budo alive, the (spiritual) way of the warrior.

The myth of this subtle energy is a field that is everything and connects everything. A field through which energy and information move, and matter is only a denser form of the same energy and information. Just like water can be ice, vapor or liquid, so the field can be information, energy or matter. Different states of the same energy. It means the universe is more a collection of frequencies than it is a collection of things.

While Embodying Reality, like my sensei does, a field of a subtle and powerful energy emerges, and a way to rediscover it is by standing still.

"When I close my eyes I discover that I am nothing. That discovery is wisdom.
When I open my eyes again, I discover that I am everything.
That discovery is love."

Nisargadatta Maharaj, Indian sage

Healing comes to you

Last year my sensei died. The unbeatable giant from Amsterdam got sick and passed away. An unknown bacteria in the hospital took the best of him. A part of reality is that all things end. All material things and ideas are temporary. Trying to hold onto things is fighting against what is. The most difficult part of connecting and staying with reality is accepting death and the end of things.

Life is full of moments of death and rebirth. Death and the end of things are the fuel for transformation. This is precisely what makes living an experience that is so full of life, as well as providing endless potential for the future. Death is the biggest life giver of all. As long as we give it the attention it deserves and allow it to be present in our lives.

Reconnecting with death and the power of letting go is essential in healing. When our imagined reality no longer matches the ever-changing reality, we become separated from reality. Like when a beloved person passes away and we have difficulty coming home to this new reality. Healing happens when we bring our imagined reality back to reality as it is. Falling into reality is healing. It's the same thing. I learned this from a healer after my encounter with death when I was fifteen.

After my physical recovery from my bicycle accident and coma, my parents were wise enough not to go right back to my old life. I was able to participate in the normal shared activities, but they didn't just want to heal the machine. They also wanted to create space for life to heal. To do this, they took me to an energetic therapist, Marijke Schneider. She helps by listening carefully to your story and then works with your energy system.

Going to Marijke is always a bit scary. She is brutally honest and sees so much before you tell her anything. You never know how she's going to respond. The only thing I know is that she makes me fall into my reality again and again, and that can be quite a shock.

One time, I think I was about 20 years old, I went to see her. First, you wait in her waiting room. You look at all the pictures of nature, indigenous people and spiritual symbols on the walls. You get called into the room and sit in front of her desk, where she sits with her notebook in front of her.

"How can I help you?" is usually the opening question. I started to explain extensively how nothing makes any sense, the world is going crazy and nobody understands me, when she suddenly hit the table as hard as she could while I was still talking. With a thunderous voice, she said: "Enough! This is your life and you have to make something of it. Get used to it!"

A bone-chilling silence ensued.

"Yes, this hurts. You can cry now."

Wayfinders give you what you need, not what you want. It taught me reality has many faces and, of course, it was very helpful in recognizing my own victimhood towards reality.

The talking is usually very short, about 5 minutes and most of the time she doesn't respond with much. Her therapy is in her energy work.

In the myth of energy work, you can consciously work with the field that connects everything. People have the ability to feel the energy, listen to the information in the field, and let it heal. In the myth of energy work, the other person's energy is the same as your own. It's already one and it's already communicating with each other. Like two different leaves from the same branch connecting with each other. Energy work is not a skill to be developed, it's connecting with what is already there.

> "The healer doesn't heal, it lets healing be."
> *Eckhart Tolle, spiritual teacher*

The purpose of energy work is to support the natural processes of the body. Treating the whole person is therefore more important than a focus on the symptoms. That's what the term 'holistic medicine' means. In energy work, you help someone with the process they're in. For some people, it cures their ailments. But, no matter the outcome, everyone grows from it.

The stories we project to the things that happen to us become part of our body. Our myth is also energy and so it also becomes part of our energy system. In energy work, there is no separation between what is real and what we make real. Conditionings are patterns from the past that have helped us. When they are no longer needed we should let them go. It's the gift of death and the end of things. In this process, energy work helps.

The more you trust life the better you become at letting go of old myths. Letting go is more than just learning to grieve, it's learning to allow reality unfold naturally. The myth that fits with it emerges by itself.

Marijke has helped me to give my accident a place, to be proud of my quick recovery and to fully unpack the gift of 'still being alive'. She has helped me to create a myth that fits my life after the accident, instead of staying stuck in what happened. Not holding on to the conditionings of the intense experience, but creating the environment in which I could let them go. Which is not a thing either of us did, it just happened. Healing comes to you.

Marijke learned this in the United States from indigenous people and, together with Barbara Brennan, she made it her own. Brennan has become world-famous with her school for healers. Marijke chose a different path.

I asked Marijke if she could teach me her energy work. She said, "Of course". I didn't know it took four years and meant to practice at home for a day every week. It was beautiful. It is - after my accident - the biggest change to my myth that I can remember.

About half way through the program, she started to teach us the exact same position of standing still that we do in Tai Ki. So the same exercise got passed on for millennia by healers in the United States, to finally find its way to her home in the Netherlands. Her framing of the exercise was that it helps you to stay on your path in life. Sounds like the way of the warrior to me.

Her teacher made her stand in this position for two hours a day during many weeks. She said five minutes a day is enough for our generation. There is much more light nowadays and we have already learned other things before we started this work. The world is quite ready for more people to connect with reality through our right hemisphere. Almost all barriers are gone, the biggest one left is the myth we live by.

In her training, the field of subtle energy gets a structure, a color, an image, a specific feeling or sensation on your hand. This is different for everyone, just as moving in Tai Ki Kenpo looks different for everyone and yet is still recognizable as the same art form.

In a treatment, you take time to listen to what the energy of the other person wants. I now describe it as connecting, listening and trusting, which does not involve any 'doing'. Still, you do a lot, but everything happens spontaneously and it feels like you're meditating together. During these healing experiences, what's in the lead is what I receive, not my techniques. You literally follow the flow of the person you're treating. You feel resonance and the rest is about trusting life.

As a healer you add 'heat' to a persons' system. By becoming warm your systems opens up and old energies can be released, restructured and finding it's way to become whole again. The same what happens in a sweat lodge, or with plant medicines. Adding heat in combination with an intention of healing is something all my wayfinders are doing.

Through practicing and having conversations with Marijke, I learned that the source of energy work is not in the techniques. Being very strict about them is therefore distracting. What matters is from what source you apply them. The grounding of good energy work is in truth, compassion and wisdom. It's about being confident about what you're doing and being fully aware that what you're doing is not so important. Reality is full of paradoxes.

Letting go of what no longer serves you allows the miracle of life to do its work. Just like, in nature restoration, you don't have to add anything. All you have to do is to be present and keep reality in the lead. Keep presencing what comes to you..

Walk away from people who promise you a path full of beautiful things. They're not connected to reality and are no wayfinders. These are people who seek followers. They usually disapprove of other wayfinders and want you to be loyal to their soft and hard systems. They're people who add a myth to your life which you must adhere to very precisely. Otherwise, things will go wrong and it will be your fault. A wayfinder, or a healer, never promises a result in advance. A wayfinder knows that he or she doesn't know it either.

The "Iron John" folk tale ends with reconciliation between the parents and the young prince at his wedding. He now becomes a king himself. A mature man has learned to be free in his connection with reality and doesn't need to be without connections in order to feel free. He can grow his kingdom and make the shared idea of "we" around him become ever greater.

In *Women Who Run with the Wolves*, the feminine version of *Iron John*, there is a fairy tale, called "Vasilisa", which is very similar to "Iron John". In this case, the feminine story about maturity does not end with a marriage. The woman walks out of the wilderness raising a staff with a skull over her head, with flames coming out of its sockets. Once she's back in the city, the skull burns everything that no longer serves life. Mature femininity is as powerful as mature masculinity, as Marijke showed me when she slammed the table with her fist. Also, mature masculinity is as intuitive and sensitive as mature femininity, as my sensei showed me when I was learning to move in a more subtle field while fighting.

When we trust life and fall into reality, we encounter as much life as we do death. We encounter as much talent as we do our shadows. As much light as darkness. This is incredibly difficult and the guidance of a wayfinder is essential here. Without the right wayfinders, we quickly step back into our familiar stories. But if we stay with what is real, healing is our reward.

*"Go into the woods.
Go into the woods.
Go into the woods.
Or never live at all."*

Clarissa Pinkola Estés, Woman who Run with the Wolves (1989)

A sense of the sacred

For a long time, I was skeptical about falling into reality with a group of people. There are so many additional obstacles in experiencing reality when we're in a group. Not just because of our own conditioning but also because groupthink can occur, as well as the extra fear of being vulnerable and upholding formal and informal roles. They all get in the way when we want to reconnect with reality as a group. I only began to trust it when I got to experience it for myself at Frank Heckman's Embassy of the Earth.

Frank has been training Tai Ki Kenpo for over forty years at the dojo where I also train. Frank has spent his entire life coaching top athletes and musicians to get into a state of flow more easily and perform at the highest level for a longer period of time. To this end, Frank has combined Joseph Campbell's Hero's Journey and Mihaly Csikszentmihalyi's work on Flow. Frank met Mihaly Csikszentmihalyi at the university of Chicago in 1992 and he became Frank's wayfinder.

> *"The most important step in emancipating oneself from social controls is the ability to find rewards in the events of each moment. If a person learns to enjoy and find meaning in the ongoing stream of experience, in the process of living itself, the burden of social control automatically falls from one's shoulders."*
>
> Mihaly Csikszentmihalyi, researcher

In 2010, Frank miraculously healed from an untreatable brain tumor with the help of a shaman in the US. It motivated Frank to set up the Embassy of the Earth. With this project, he travels to places where people experience most intensely the existential challenges of climate change every day: the indigenous people of many different countries. These communities have become fragmented by ecological decay, and he helps them restore their social fabric.

By reconnecting to landscape restoration, they themselves are once again organized and connected with each other. Restoring the landscape is the goal and strengthening the community is the means. In this way, nature restoration and community healing become the same process.

The theory they use for this is based on the process of a 'search conference', developed by Merrelyn and Fred Emery, which they passed on to Frank. Since 2019, Frank has been teaching this method to a group of people in the Netherlands, and I was one of the lucky individuals who got to participate in his program to become a social architect.

A search conference is a process of making a plan with a community in such a way that ownership over the plan is completely with the community. It's a process of making a plan together that generates as much human energy as possible. There are no outside experts present. There are no presentations. There is a host who keeps an eye on the process and the time, but other than that, everyone is just working.

There is a puzzle-solving focus in doing carefully selected tasks. The participants spend most of the time talking to each other to deliver a certain output. Like, "What would the world look like if we don't act?" and "What is the history of our group?"

In having those conversations, there are a number of principles that provide direction. The first and perhaps most important one is that everyone leaves their hat at the door. That is, leaving your function at the door to participate as a person. "How do you, as a person, feel about this question?" This leaves the myth which we have in a certain job position at the door, and everyone contributes to the idea of reality by sharing what their imagined reality is. All perspectives are welcome and when it comes to ownership over a plan, authority is a hindrance.

When people engage in dialogue as equals and share what they experience as essential in the world, it produces a magical effect. The human energy generated in a search conference is unprecedented. It not only produces a supported plan, but it also improves the capacity of the participants in "active adaptation." It means to put reality at the center on a daily basis. A core skill when it comes to staying with reality in turbulent times.

The path to reality that I learned from search conferences is an open dialogue between people in which they talk about what is essential to them. Once groupthink, the modern myth, or someone's position gets in the way, it's no longer a dialogue but a discussion about who's telling the best story about the world. A search conference is as exciting and transformative as a wild path. You learn to see with new eyes and with a whole group at the same time.

One of the secret ingredients of a search conference is the creation of sacred ground. Creating sacred ground is something we have been doing since we started organizing ourselves based on myths. It's a place, a ceremony, a ritual, in which everyone that is present has their attention on the same thing. I don't mean everyone obediently watching, but a situation in which everyone is involved in the same thing with their whole being. Lighting a candle, singing a song, dancing together and handing over something from person to person are actions often used in order to achieve this. On sacred ground, it's possible for a whole group to walk through the gate at the same time and step into the unknown.

> *"That, I think, is the power of ceremony: it marries the mundane to the sacred. The water turns to wine, the coffee to a prayer. The material and the spiritual mingle... What else can you offer the earth which has everything? What else can you give but something of yourself? A homemade ceremony, a ceremony that makes home."*
>
> Robin Wall Kimmerer in Braiding Sweetgrass, 2013

I saw for myself what sacred ground does during a survival trip with a group of twenty friends in a forest. Everyone was asked to bring something with which they could present their soul animal to the group. At the campfire, after a day of adventure in the woods and some delicious food, someone gave the first impetus. "Now it's time for everyone to present their soul animal. If anyone is ready, they may step into the circle." Everyone shared their story and everyone was respectful with each other, even people who had nothing to do with it, or did not yet know their soul animal. Nothing is as magical as a group of people around the campfire sharing what is essential to them.

Sacred ground is a container in which everybody is focusing on something real. Something happening at that very moment.

What I learned from being at this campfire with friends is that, on sacred ground, everything is seen and everything is OK. Everything that happens in that moment is exactly what needs to happen. You experience the heat of the group's attention, but also unconditional acceptance. This also means that, if you start confabulating or making up stories, the group will let you know. It's precisely the unfiltered presence of everyone that ensures that the connection with compassion is not lost. Which also immediately shows the fragility of sacred ground. If someone steps out of this respectful attitude, starts whispering to somebody, or chuckles softly in the background, the sacred ground immediately disappears. This means everyone is no longer in the moment with their whole being, and therefore the feeling of unconditional acceptance is broken. When this happens, there are stories being shared that not everybody is connecting to.

At the same time, sacred ground is precisely the place where people are powerful. On sacred ground, everything is OK and everything that happens is also the only thing that could happen. Even a sincere response such as: "What a bad story", which is something that came up regularly at the campfire with my friends. In a normal social environment, this would have been hurtful, but someone on sacred ground can handle that just fine. It is what it is.

When we fall into reality and are in the moment together with our whole being, there is room to just talk to each other and there is no longer the endless list of things you have to take into account in order not to hurt anyone. In open and equal dialogues between people at search conferences, I have seen myths change.

I've seen the same happen on sacred ground. When everyone has their focus on something real, then myths become grounded once again.

The modern world is so far from reality it has lost its sense of what is sacred, in the same way it has lost its feeling for subtle energy and knowledge about healing. Nathaniel Altmant tries to make us feel what is sacred once again through his descriptions of sacred trees. Sacred trees have played a central part in community life in nearly every human culture. His book *Sacred Trees* tells us why a tree can be called sacred by the people who live with it. It can be easily translated to other parts of our life to rediscover the sacred:

> *The tree provides an essential product or service to the community. If it's sacred, it doesn't mean we don't kill it.*
> *The tree is located near a sacred river, spring, or well.*
> *A tree as a land marker.*
> *The tree is connected to a sacred animal that lives in or from the tree. Like owls, hawks, or bees.*
> *The tree is connected to a significant historical event. A war, a wedding, dispensing justice or negotiating a treaty.*
> *The tree is associated with the appearance of a spirit being. Through certain trees we can connect more easily to other dimensions.*

The tree may have a special power for healing, purification or enlightenment.

The tree's location is near a place of worship, ceremony, or purification rituals. It can also work the other way around. When a place of worship is created near a sacred tree.

A tree can be distinct in some way from others of its species. Very old, or unusually large.

The tree can be a symbol of fertility, or aid the growth of crops. In the classic story of a stork bringing a baby to its parents, the source of the baby is a local children-tree and the stork does the delivery.

Learning to communicate with nature and learning to view the world from the perspective of nature is called 'deep ecology'. It's based on an old idea that everything in nature is interconnected and alive. Or as James Lovelock describes it: people and everything else on the planet, are parts of one huge organism, called Gaia. Focusing our attention on what is sacred opens our reductionist minds and makes us fall into reality again. Anything that is real by itself is sacred, important and primary in life. Anything we make real we can change and is secondary in life.

Frank calls falling into reality: "Coming home to earth again." He graduated from dance academy and loves to perform, and loves to invite others to perform as well. "In performing we learn the most, but it's also the place we fear the most." He embodies the miracle of life, by inviting people to enter a state of flow. Through the intensity of performing and doing ceremonies, a certain 'heat' is added which is necessary for the healing experience to take place.

> "We are the consciousness of the world. What else?"
>
> *Joseph Campbell, writer*

Living from wisdom

Finding your way closer to reality is what Jaap Voigt has built his career on. Through a good friend of Tai Ki Kenpo, I came across Jaap's I Ching and Dao de Jing programs. Four evenings practicing with the Chinese *Book of Changes*, the *I Ching*; and four evenings practicing with the Chinese book of what is unchangeable in life, the *Dao de Jing*. Both Chinese books have been translated into Dutch by Jaap. Along with his books and guidance, you learn to translate this ancient philosophy to your daily life.

I was hungry for more and, for the past six years, I have regularly met with Jaap, along with a group of people, to talk about Eastern philosophy and how to translate it to our daily lives. As friends, we talk about what is essential to us.

Jaap has a long career behind him and has seen much of the world. During his life, he started by playing for the Dutch national hockey team, then worked at Philips, he was an urban planner, an organizational consultant, spent many years in Israel for peace building purposes, he stayed in an Ashram in northern India for seven years and also wrote several books. Although his work has been about many different things, it has always been about focusing on what is real.

I know him as a writer about Eastern philosophies and somebody who you consult when you try to do anything meaningful in life. He knows how difficult it is to stay with what is real and how lonely this road can be. Focusing on real things brings you meaning. Focusing on what we make real brings confusion.

Exploring your imagined reality with Jaap feels like someone is shining a flashlight through your consciousness. Everything is touched for a moment. After a one-on-one conversation, or an afternoon with a group, you walk out with a grounded myth. Time seems to disappear during these moments and anything can be shared. Nothing special really happens, but it still feels extraordinary.

Whereas the other wayfinders have a technique for conveying their healing, with Jaap it comes from the art of living itself. There is no energy work, martial arts or search conferences to talk about. There is just human contact. A certain interaction in which your whole humanity is allowed to be present.

Like the other wayfinders, Jaap is compassionate and frighteningly honest at the same time. You don't know in advance what you're going to be confronted with, or how you're going to walk out. Every interaction with a wayfinder is like sacred ground. Everything is seen and everything is OK.

In our conversations with Jaap, there has always been philosophical content and a moment of silence, although, most of the time, the subject is usually centered on what's happening in our daily lives. We don't go looking for problems or endless conversations about how we think things should be. But we try to allow reality to be as it is, and sharing that with the group is usually enough. Jaap's attention and language provide that little extra bit of support and grip on the process you're in. No matter how unpleasant the myth you're trapped in is, grounding it once again provides relief.

Working with what happens in our daily lives is endlessly profound. Becoming a part of reality also means being able to view the big world problems in a personal light. Being able to translate them into the now, learning to deal with what we see in the world and bringing that realization to our own lives without putting global crises on our shoulders. We're not going to solve them, but we shouldn't ignore them either, thinking someone else is going to solve them for us.

On a wild path, what we find anew is healing, wisdom, subtle fields of energy and a new sense of what is sacred. We become smart and intelligent in our trust systems. But these qualities are dependent on our myth. We learn what wisdom is from things that are real. And wisdom is independent of our myth. We find it by falling into reality and working on our addictions. Wisdom is about keeping things real and we learn it from real things. Jaap is the embodiment of this. His heart's desire for the world is to be mundane again.

If we succeed in keeping things real, we create space for intense experiences in which our myth can ground itself once again. For example, in moments of sadness, sometimes I don't want to cry out of shame. Then, all my attention goes to not crying and there's less of an intense experience in which a myth can be grounded. Overwriting your own humanity with willpower is possible, but it becomes an obstacle for keeping things real.

Another example is not wanting to share your opinion in a meeting. If you have an opinion about something and you don't share it, you're creating an energy leak. Also, you're much less likely to get, or give, an intense experience, and so everyone in that meeting misses an opportunity to ground their myth. If you don't share your imagined reality, no one will be able to participate in a complete shared reality.

From the books of Jan Geurtz, an addiction therapist, I learned beautiful words for breaking free from our addictions and healing. If we don't know we're addicted, then we're entangled in our idea of reality. We walk in one world, thinking we know reality and what's the right thing to do. But that's like continuing to hope for 'the system' to solve global crises. That is, we remain in the modern myth.

When we recognize that we're addicted, we want to be free of it and start to dissociate. We begin to resist the addiction and, by doing so, we make it grow. We become self-critical about being judgmental. We get busy trying to relax more. We say 'sorry' for saying 'sorry' too much. We start convincing other people to get out of a colonizing myth. We control ourselves in order to not control anything.

Dissociation is finding Iron John, but putting him in a cage.

This happens quite frequently with sustainability. If we try to work on sustainability but keep humans at the center, it's very tempting to start making new stories, technologies and legislation, and try to convince other people to follow them. Which will only get us further away from reality and make life more complicated instead of more real.

Dissociation is also claiming you become stronger from trauma. It's seeing the miracle of life, but putting it in a story once again. By claiming this, you assume control over life and implicitly tell people they should get stronger from the trauma they have gone through. The miracle of life allows us to get stronger from trauma, but making it a goal is narrowing the possibility, not favoring it.

Dissociation is also putting your well-being first. It's recognizing the modern paradigm grants very little importance to our own health. Most people in the modern world die because of their own lifestyle, which we think is normal because of our paradigm. The modern myth exploits our bodies, as it exploits the world we live in. But putting your own health above anything else separates you from reality again. It's falling into another extreme instead of finding a way to get better.

Dissociation is also understanding that sustainability needs healing and healing is something you have to do yourself. When you start putting the responsibility for everything that happens in your life on your own shoulders, you've gone to the other extreme. The modern myth is very good in acting as if caring for the whole is not a responsibility we have. But acting as if everything that happens to you is your own fault is the other extreme. You're responsible for your reaction to life, you're not responsible for what happens to you.

In order to step out of this dissociation phase, we must allow reality to be as it is. It's about acknowledging that we're critical, that we say 'sorry' too much and that we're too busy tackling the issue of sustainability from the old myth's perspective. In reality we find truth, compassion and wisdom. But we can also fall into reality by starting to look for truth, (self-)compassion and wisdom.

To do so, we must allow what is to be, accept reality as it is, without judgment and without running to another extreme. The complete opposite of what we consider to be 'the wrong normal' is still a story of how things should be. The meaning of life is living, not doing good. Most of the angry farmers, truckers and conspiracy extremists are in the dissociating phase. A necessary step, but not an example of where the solution lies.

They feel that what is happening in the modern world doesn't make any sense, but what they propose is making things even worse. Especially, those that brandish the argument that there is no problem to begin with. That's typical left hemisphere thinking. Ignoring reality and living in their own bubble, like the modern myth they are attempting to fight. Another similar argument states that there is no truth, or there is no reality. Both Jaap

Voigt and Iain McGilchrist are strong advocates for making it very clear that there is only one reality and one truth. You just can't claim it, because it is a movement, a process and entangled with it's observer.

The key is to allow everything to be. It's the reason why surrendering, grounding, intention, connecting and trusting are helping the transformation process the world is currently in. And why planning, predicting, controlling, acting, using and storytelling are not so helping.

Being smart means you know things. Being intelligent means you know how to do things. Being wise means you know when to use them. Jaap embodies this. He embodies the balance between acting in the world and developing your inner world. Jaap dedicated his life in helping others find their balance and preserving wisdom for future generations. A guardian of the spiritual way.

> *"When we step into the unknown, what needs healing comes to light."*
>
> Jaap Voigt, wisdom keeper

A mystery

The first conscious choice I made that I can remember is wanting to learn how to play drums. Through a local music school, I met Loui Blom. A real theatrical drummer and a creative genius. Although he gets annoyed when you call it 'being creative'. He says it's just being. He got the same nickname as my sensei, The Beast. One time, he took an enormous steel washing tub with him on stage, into which he occasionally broke an empty bottle of wine while playing. "Everyone went crazy, it was beautiful."

He built an insulated studio in his attic for when he teaches. On the way up, you can see a lot of African art. He's a big fan of African drummers, because that's where drumming originated. The story he shares about how a drum set came to be, is that it used to be an entire tribe, but now is just one person playing one instrument. In the US, they put all those different percussion instruments together into what we know as a drum set today, so one person could play them and so it could fit on a stage. A drummer is a "one-man tribe."

The first thing Loui always asks me upon entering the studio is if I want fries and a beer. Once in the studio with our beer and fries, there are two drum sets waiting for us. We usually start by taking turns playing a four-bar solo, while the other keeps a normal rhythm. After four bars, we switch over and keep doing that until we've had enough. So sometimes I play a fixed rhythm for four bars to support him while he does his solo, and sometimes I play a solo myself and he supports me.

A solo means that you play freely and let your drum sticks move over the drums and cymbals. Not thinking, not planning, but just talking with your drum sticks, as if you're telling a story together. You don't want to be overly technical or make a plan for your next solo, you just want to play what emerges in the moment.

Of course, sometimes I try to make a plan or want to play technically, but it never works. It's too much information to deal with while playing freely. Your conscious mind can't handle all that. You just make mistakes and keep going. But if I manage to combine total surrender and total presence, then sometimes I manage to just play. And the vibe of playing from total surrender is pure gold.

Loui's feedback when I'm stumbling is, "Relax your shoulders," or "Give each stroke meaning," or "Don't try to do anything complicated, just play." All I get is timeless, universal feedback. Things that are always true and are actually quite impersonal.

Yet, it's usually exactly what I need to hear in that moment. He expresses so much confidence in me, while also being both clear and confrontational. Giving feedback in this way is something all my wayfinders do. They give feedback without adding a story that wasn't already there. They share timeless principles which you can make your own, rather than giving you instructions on how things should be done. This is how you learn their craft without losing your individuality. Universal truths don't complicate life, they lead the way to a deep and simple life.

The modern myth makes the whole secondary, struggles against death, puts nature very far away from people, and interprets humanity very narrowly, and it gives social status to pretending you understand and control life. So much so that we often perceive it as mature to pretend to know how life works. But if there's anything timeless, it's that we will never fully understand reality. Reality is much more of a mystery than a collection of things.

How the world works, who we are, who the other is, why we are here, where a decision comes from, where trust comes from, what our consciousness is and what intelligence is, are all questions that we will probably never have a comprehensive answer to. We may be able to understand an increasingly larger system or describe smaller and smaller particles, but understanding all of reality is not what we were made for. Everything has its reasons, but understanding all the reasons is not a prerequisite for a good life. Reality is and always will be a mystery.

Everything that we have ever discovered started with accepting that we don't know something yet. Every time you have learned something, it's because you started from the fact that you did not know everything. Not knowing is wonderful, liberating and essential to feeling comfortable in turbulent times. Not knowing is a prerequisite for living fully. Not knowing is delightful, until you ruin it with the myth that it's not such a delight.

In the modern myth, we have been made to fear 'not knowing' while rewarding 'being sure of everything'. Knowing gives us power because the myth gives it attention. We act as if having a goal and achieving this goal is the best way to live. And so we act as if predicting the future is essential to having a good life. Whereas not knowing is a prerequisite for our best experience: to flow.

Moments of spontaneity, laughter, new ideas, inspiration, improvisation, creating art, really listening during a conversation and sharing intimate healing moments, these are some of the best experiences we can have and they all come from not knowing. They happen when we trust the mystery of life over our own story about life.

When we know how to trust the mystery and dare to step confidently into the unknown, we find an enormous source of creativity, joy and connection. Not knowing is associated, by the modern paradigm, with doubt. However, not knowing is also the source of improvisation and spontaneity. To flow is also to not know what is going to happen. To walk through the gate is to step into the mystery. It grounds our myths, and how that even works is a mystery as well.

When we're uncomfortable with not-knowing, we get a chance to learn how to trust life more. When we lose our job, a relationship, or a loved one gets sick, we don't know what's going to happen. Whoever learns to live with uncertainty becomes wise. It's our connection to mystery that ultimately has an effect on our myth. How it works no one knows. What it requires is for us to trust in life.

Not knowing is the space the wayfinders create by playing freely on a drum, by fighting, by creating sacred ground, or through energy work and wisdom. It's about reconnecting people with the mystery which every moment holds.

Now, because reality is a mystery, following these chapters on reality is not what reality is truly about. To put energy, healing, wisdom and what is sacred into a story and start being orthodox about it, is to put Iron John in a cage and stop listening to reality. Reality is moving, ever changing and has no fixed state. Any concept about reality is not what reality is all about. A concept is always a trust system, with its own thinking bubble, and therefore not the whole, in the same way language can never completely capture reality. It's about what the language points to.

Now I can summarize falling into reality in one word: Being. Being is my answer. My answer for grounding myths, falling into reality, working on a new paradigm for sustainability, living with the paradoxes of reality and dealing with an endlessly complex and ever changing reality.

This brings a certain simplicity back to this new domain of working on myths. Love, truth, mystery, reality, life, death, wisdom, justice and being are different words describing the same. Why not give it one word: God? Everything that is.

Now I also understand how all five wayfinders can exemplify all of reality. They don't fill them with a list of how things should be, because that would quickly become a very complicated life. They live from simply being and therefore become an example of every expression of reality.

This reminds me of a moment I shared with an old woman in Iran. I was buying ice cream at an ice-cream parlor near the main square of Isfahan. Isfahan is the city in which the fairy tale Aladdin occurs. And that's just how magical that square is. The woman was wearing a beautiful light blue headscarf and had a tanned, wrinkled face full of life experiences. Her bright blue eyes looked at me deeply, yet calmly. She spoke surprisingly good English, so I assumed she had seen a lot of the world. After some small talk, I asked her what it was like to live as a woman in Iran. With a twinkle in her eyes, she said: "The sky is blue everywhere."

While visiting Iran, we traveled mostly during the night by bus, so we could see as much as possible during the day. One night we stopped at a small gas station for a break and we got out to buy some snacks. Inside, above the entrance, there was a big poster of an enormous tree. It said: "Oldest tree in the Middle East, 4500 years old".

I was dumbstruck. Nothing in me deemed it possible that trees could be that old. Imagine all the things it has witnessed in 4500 years. Imagine all the weather changes and human influences it adapted to. Reality truly is so much more than our ideas about it. In such moments, I feel fire glowing in my bones.

A quick Google search confirmed the message. There is a 4000 to 4500-year-old tree standing in the province of Yazd in East Iran. It even has a name: Zoroastrian Sarv, meaning Cypress of Abarkuh. And I learned there are many more millennia-old trees around the world. The calling was clear, a seed had been planted.

For writing this book, I used the very message of the book as my method. That is, writing it as it emerges, then reading it back to check if it was any good. Presencing in the lead and structure as a way to make it shareable with others. A very scary, but healing process. In the beginning, I knew I had a story to tell, but I didn't have the words for it. I clearly had another vision on sustainability than most *of the people in the sustainability movement, but I didn't have the words to describe it. Knowing without thinking is a good indicator for identifying information coming from our right hemisphere.*

When I started to write, I soon found myself being fascinated by our myths and the power of humans. I continued writing a new story for sustainability, calling it a global paradigm, an ecological mind and other new concepts. Somewhere I knew it wasn't right, but at first I didn't know why. Then I realized I was doing the same thing that I judge the modern myth for doing. Trying to colonize the minds of the readers of how sustainability should be done. Writing this book as it emerged was a process for me to explain to my left hemisphere it shouldn't be in the lead. Sustainability needs a new paradigm that is grounded in reality. A paradigm gets roots when we fall into reality. A new story before we fall into reality only gets in the way.

In order to see reality as it is, concepts and solutions are a distraction. We're not going to think ourselves out of this mess. Just as you don't think yourself out of a burnout, or any other illness. You surrender to it, start seeing yourself as part of the problem and return to simply being from truth, (self-) compassion and wisdom.

When I got stuck and the words didn't flow anymore, I

reimagined the wonder I felt when learning about these ancient trees. Then I interviewed them, asked them my questions and wrote down their answers. Many times they gave me the courage and content to continue. It inspired me to go on a journey around the world and visit the oldest living trees and forests. To honor them and learn what lives there that cannot be planted.

I published this book in Dutch in the summer of 2021. After which I bought a converted German fire truck from 1981 and started this amazing journey. For a little over a year, I've traveled to visit the most old, big, weird and remarkable trees and forests. First in the Netherlands, then France and Italy and now in North-America.

The trees taught me they're that old because we have included them into our culture and trust system. They're sacred trees, monumental trees, and historic trees. What we make real should be as close as possible to what is real. Facilitating a natural life in harmony with all of creation.

The path of the black sheep

Traveling near Quebec, Canada, I met Little Half-Moon, also known as Mike. He is a Medewin elder. He's walking, together with his partner Liane from the east coast of Nova Scotia, in Canada, to the west coast of California, in the US. A two-year journey, where each day begins and ends with a ceremony. They are building a spirit lodge for Turtle Island (North-America). Making space for the spirits to do their work. They sleep in a converted ambulance, so the match with our fire truck was easily made.

They walk for healing purposes and reconnecting with the divine masculine and feminine. While walking Mike sings his songs, says his prayers and talks with the plants and animals. He tells very few people about his journey, as he's walking for the spirits.

He believes that only the spirits can do meaningful work now. He renounced all formal positions within his community, because he sees it as just another structure, dogma and distraction. Now that you're reading the final chapter of the book, I'm sure you already know we both connected instantly.

When you step out of the structure you're familiar with and start to live from the whole, you quickly become the black sheep of your community. The power of humans needs uniformity and loyalty to the same story. People who live from a different story are quickly seen as a threat.

Black sheeps are Embodying Reality, or at least on a road to be able to do so. For them, each day is a wild path. Their very existence is a threat to the current system, but they don't fight the system because they know that convincing people doesn't help. You can't change the system by fighting it. Just like you also can't change the system from the inside. Black sheeps live as much as possible outside of the system and trust life as much as they can. They live in a balance between inner and outer work, understanding there is not much difference between the two anyway. And they avoid the extremes, knowing reality is about balance and opposites that need each other.

The good thing about Embodying Reality as a new paradigm for sustainability is that a lot of people are already doing it and even more are trying to do it (in the dissociation phase). They realize that optimizing the system with partial sustainability solutions so that we can keep our old paradigm is a very disappointing path. You never seem to be doing enough and real life examples are very scarce, if not completely nonexistent. The old paradigm about sustainability invites endless discussions about which system optimization is the best (for other people), with very little real action. Like the Paris Accords.

Embodying Reality is something that's happening a lot already. People doing this start to prioritize the whole over the parts. They don't separate themselves from the whole, or try to do good by adding things to a wrong system. They reconnect with the whole through real things: food, water, air, soil, nature, life, death, health, passions, talents. They're relearning that what is real is important and primary in life. And what we make real can be changed and is secondary. Coming home to what is. As soon as you reverse your priorities and start to prioritize what is real, our culture and legislation drop you as if you are scolding hot. You become the black sheep of your community.

Adding good things to our outdated foundation is not helping, we need a new foundation. Like more budgets, more technology, or new legislation. It are good things to do, but with the wrong foundation it won't be enough.

A new foundation for our future is made by radical people. The origin of the word radical is 'radix', which means 'root' and 'ground'. People who have reality in the lead are radical people. Things are coming to light as never before and it's challenging everybody to rethink their entire worldview. Including the foundation we base our lives on. New roots is what we need. We need each other and we need to get out of our shared paradigm at the same time.

Embodying Reality is an including path. It's not against anything that is already happening. It is an acceleration of what is happening by focusing on healing instead of convincing. Whatever it is you're doing, how can you move from doing it for love to doing it from love? From convincing to healing. How can you enhance our trust in life by what you're already doing?

Real life examples are the most telling. During the past year, I have spoken with a few of them. Radical people who focus on what is real and help others to connect with reality as well. Without excluding the modern world as it is today. Here are three examples.

Nicky Leidelmeijer is a holistic nutritionist and offers her services in the same building as my crossfit box was. When I started to write this book, I started to do more sports and eat healthier, but I didn't become fitter. I ate fresh, diverse and healthy things on a regular basis, so my imagined reality was 100% sure I was doing good already. It felt like a smart algorithm.

With Nicky's help, I found out I ate 66% of the calories I needed and 50% of the protein I needed. My reality was that I had been hungry for decades. I ate healthy except for one thing: quantity. My conditioning was so strong it overwrote my natural feeling for hunger with ease.

When my stress of having a busy modern life fell away by starting to write, I had the space to stand still and notice what was really happening. By eating more, I became fitter again. Nicky taught me that some people start eating because of stress, others forget to eat because of stress.

She did not force me on a diet through willpower. Instead she started asking me: How do you want to live? What works for you already? What food do you like? She did this slowly, based on reality, without wanting to control or force anything.

She told me the entire food industry is focused on getting

consumers addicted to their food. In developed countries, our food is optimized for addiction, not for nutrition. In helping her clients, her two biggest obstacles are almost all the products found in the supermarket, and the social dynamic we have with normalizing drinking alcohol.

Her way to go about it is to measure what is really happening, showing her clients what they put in their bodies, through blood tests and measuring their body metrics regularly. Then she helps them with knowledge, sometimes a stern correction, but always a lot of compassion during every step.

She didn't dive into 'proven' quick solutions, but rather let the solution grow from my own life. A holistic approach. In order for the change in eating patterns to be durable, everything in my life had to support it. That also meant emotions, thoughts, desires, habits and goals, everything that emerges must be taken seriously into consideration. This is a phenomenological approach: seeing what emerges.

A path to a new paradigm for sustainability is very much the same. The guidance and leadership I needed for it seemed to be right around the corner as soon as I started to write about it.

Susanne Duijvesteijn-de Boer was a successful banker, working on a sustainability portfolio. She fell into reality after she became a mother. As she started asking herself the difficult questions of life, she realized her reality didn't match with corporate business. Her reality was about a major topic that had always fascinated her: death. She became a holistic funeral director and a black sheep in an extremely commercial and conservative sector.

For five years now, she has helped reimagine funerals in a way they become part of a healing process. She creates emotional and spiritual space for people to reconnect with reality while mourning a beloved one. She does this by asking the right questions, opening space for silence and pointing out to them that they can design a funeral in almost any way they want. In her process she heartily includes the healing of Mother Earth.

Susanne is deeply grounded in the knowledge you cannot heal yourself separately from Mother Earth. They go hand in hand and are inseparable. Mother Earth brings us the miracle of life that is needed for healing in the first place.

She encourages a death shroud over a coffin because a coffin is full of plastics and chemicals. Therefore, she also encourages natural clothing because usually our clothing is also full of plastic and chemicals. She encourages natural embalming to preserve the body, because the body's blood is usually replaced with chemicals in order for the body to look better in death.

These are things we are allowed to choose in order to improve how we do things. But to make a funeral a process that's fully a part of life on our planet, she faced the obstacle that it's illegal to do it this way. In the modern myth, we are not allowed to deal with death in a natural way.

Both cremation and burial are not things that happen in the

real world. It takes a lot of energy to burn a body, and when you bury someone, the body has to be buried six feet underground where there is no life to actually digest the body. To compost a body, letting it return organically to the soil, is not allowed in the modern world.

She wrote a book about reimagining funerals as a healing process. In the book, she completely destroys her own sector, showing how commercial, heartless and unsustainable it has become, including the legislation which forbids a natural funeral. She also does this by sharing inspirational alternatives and rituals, highlighting natural material use and outdoor gatherings, opening possibilities in order to say our goodbyes in a healing way.

She can do this because she *is* her work. She brings her whole being and she doesn't sugarcoat anything. She deals with death as it is, from the whole to the parts.

Mark Tigchelaar worked all over the world with the leaders of the largest corporations. He was always asked for the most difficult cases because he always found a way to a solution. His areas of expertise are leadership and transformation. There is no official list for it, but it's reasonable to say Mark was one of the best and most wanted consultants in the world.

He is also a world-class ocean sailor, spending as much time as possible at sea during his twenties. He used his sailing experience in business, for high performance teamwork and deep dialogue sessions. He was able to improve performance wherever he went by 200% or 300%, instead of the usual 10% or 20%.

He was asked to do the most difficult cases because he has always been a black sheep. Even when he was a consultant in an international firm, he was never part of the system. This allowed him to see doorways and paths in situations where nobody else could see any.

> *"That which has no form can enter where there is no opening."*
>
> Lao Tzu, Dao de Jing (about 500 BC)

His strategy was to be more successful in the old paradigm by bringing the new paradigm. As brilliant as this is, it's often not very durable, as the participants are easily blinded by the success it creates and therefore miss the reason for this success: a grounded, flowing, unfolding paradigm. Mark saw his creations, a new consultancy, numerous organizations he helped and leadership programs he started, lose their essence over the years. And this caused a giant like Mark to fall into reality by burning out.

The man that could work for almost any organization in the world, for any amount of money he desired, decided to focus on his biggest challenge: to feel at home. Now he's the example of new leadership by working on his house, his health, his boat and his relationships. Building a new foundation for the world can also start in your own living room. He now coaches a small circle of pioneers into finding new doorways from a deeper state of being. Focusing on what is real has a global effect, no matter which scale you work on.

For his billion-dollar-budget friends, Mark is the black sheep. He threatens their story of success by his mere existence. The power of non-doing.

"Standing still is an essential act of creation and growth. In the real world of consciousness, infinite pathways towards a future are opened. In our beings, qualities and capabilities of transformative leadership are being crafted. While in the real world, healing begins inevitably at the moment we stop aggravating the damage to the whole."

Mark Tigchelaar, ocean sailor

Nicky, Suzanne and Mark stepped away from their imagined reality, reconnected with reality, stopped adding to the problem and allowed the miracle of life to do its work. Now they guide others in doing the same. The results are new roots, a new foundation on which a new myth can emerge. This kind of work is exactly what sustainability needs, it's just not currently called sustainability. Working from the whole to the parts, instead of trying to manage the whole from the parts up.

If I integrate everything I learned from these radical people as well as my wayfinders, the process of curing a body seems to be a great metaphor: 1. Understanding the(re is a) problem 2. Removing the cause 3. Creating the conditions for the body to heal. 4. Trust life.

I explain them here for humanity as a whole, but they also hold true for your own life as well as for specific groups of people.

Understanding the(re is a) problem. If we start taking global crises seriously and start responding to them for the threat that they are, we would immediately stop adding to the problem. Something we can only do when we understand we are the problem and we're not busy adding 'solutions' to a wrong system.

An important part of being realistic is being proportional. Our reaction to global crises should be proportional to the threat they present. This will only happen when we have an intense reaction to it, something that make us see the importance of the situation and opens our eyes to its cause: *We are the problem.*

And this can even happen overnight, like when a war erupts or a natural disaster occurs. Myths can change in an instant and often do. But more likely it will take more time. People who are entangled in their idea about reality are impossible to convince. They need healing, not convincing. The first step for this is to stop adding things to the wrong system and call them solutions. It needs space so life (the spirits) can do the work.

Let's take one political term, four yours, for this important part of the process towards a new paradigm for sustainability. A four-year ban on adding anything to a wrong foundation, a ban on doing non-essential things, four years of non-doing. Which isn't the same as doing nothing. We still need food, sleep, a house, health and time with loved ones. But it does mean to stop wanting things we don't need and to stop exploiting the whole in order to obtain them. Four years of healing from our addictions and falling into reality together. So we can come to the deep realization; the problem and thus the solution, is inside ourselves.

Understanding "we are the problem" is the most important and the most difficult part of this process. It's the step in which we wake up from the hypnosis of our own myth. This will need a lot of stillness, openness and patience in order to allow everything that is. Four years of non-doing.

Without this step it's easy to keep our left hemisphere in the lead. Claiming there is no truth, or no reality, or science is just an opinion, and keep adding things to a wrong system. In other words, we stay in our self-conforming bubble.

Removing the causes. Step two is all about going forward by removing things, or *via negativa,* as the Stoics call it. The study of what not to do. We can only do this properly when we start from wisdom, from the whole. Therefore healing is step one and we start with four years of non-doing.

The goal here is to search for things that could be removed so we're no longer distracted from the fact that reality should be primary in our lives, not secondary. I refer to the ideas in our mental landscape that keep us believing that our imagined realities are more important than reality itself. Open dialogues are a great tool for this.

Having open dialogues about land ownership, country borders, making money with money, and economic growth as an overriding purpose, just to state a few. How do they still serve reality today? And how do they contribute to solving our greatest problems?

Also, other issues open to dialogue are: the food in our supermarkets, the incentives in our healthcare system, the idea of success in education, the maximum allowed size of financial and commercial organizations, and do we still need the concept of a pension for people's well-being? Do these concepts still serve reality?

The low-hanging fruit is to stop investing in fossil fuels and to stop increasing credit to counter credit crises. So to stop doing what we have been doing during the past few decades. Suppressing symptoms instead of solving the causes. Patches work for the short term because we trust them, but it keeps us in the wrong myth and diminishes the potential of our future.

One step further is to look more closely at our current system. We could, for example, stop granting organizations limited responsibility. Now we create legal entities that do not exist in reality and give them limited responsibility. A Dutch invention by the way.

We allow the most powerful made-up entities on the planet to have less liabilities. Like all the companies on the stock exchange. Of course, they should have more responsibilities, not less.

After limiting their liability, we add all kinds of rules to ask these huge organizations to take more responsibilities in order to improve fair wages, do their environmental reporting and start ethical production chains, for example. But this is contradictory and, currently, they show very few results in these aspects because their paradigm currently states: "We are not responsible". And they're right. We grant big corporations limited liability while asking them to take on more responsibilities, which makes no sense. So far, when it comes to sustainability, we've mostly been adding good things to a wrong foundation. This needs to stop, we must first create a more realistic foundation. Which doesn't feel like the acceleration it is, if we do not first come to the realization; we are the problem.

Furthermore, so much of the current economy can just be erased. It's almost all fantasy numbers anyway. Money should not be allowed to accumulate, its purpose is to circulate. Now money is just giving scared rich people the illusion of safety. If it does not contribute to something real, let's make it disappear. It's just one decision away.

Removing the causes, step two, should be done ruthlessly, like a hot knife through butter. The same way removing a tumor from a body is done. Surgical and clean. So what needs to be created, to facilitate this process, is an indisputable strength that has no interest in power over others.

Mike has told me indigenous people can do this. They have Embodied Reality forever and some of them still live outside of our made-up reality and have an open myth about the world. Mike has told me that the role of "the red man" (indiginous) is to guide humanity and bring all "colors of man" back together. I believe they have the wisdom and strength to do this.

Creating the conditions for the body to heal. Without the festering tumors of old paradigms in our mental landscape, we can enjoy the miracle of life together. So many good things happen from just being present and following what is. Ecosystems regenerate, bodies balance, relationships heal, food grows, children mature. Let's disturb that as little as possible. Like the first rule of curing a body: do not do harm.

Healing happens when we connect with what is real. When we stop acting from how things should be. You cannot connect with reality past your own shortcomings. Healing is moving from living for love to living from love. The first step in creating conditions for our collective to heal is to start with where you are now. The more you fall into reality, the more you heal. Where you automatically make it easier for other people to do this as well. We make the path by walking.

The force of sitting with what is and non-doing is enormous, although it can be confusing for the modern mind to understand that non-doing is not the same as doing nothing. It's not apathy, it can be very active. You just stay in the flow of life instead of working from a story. It's the same as how energy work is performed: connecting, listening, trusting. It's like what I shared about telling a story by playing the drums from a state of surrender. Or like fighting somebody from a state of relaxed alertness by moving in a field of energy.

The right conditions to do this are different everywhere. But to have an open mind and an open heart seems to be the most universal principle of all. Be present, share your truth, and listen to the truth of other people, as well as listen to your own myth. You find your myth by looking at how you experience the world. Because how you experience the world says more about your own myth than it says about the world.

Trusting life. At every turn of this path towards a new paradigm, it's very easy to let the ego slip in and take over. Claiming truths, creating concepts, building hierarchies and rejecting certain types of people and opinions. Bringing us back to a state of separation. Trusting life keeps the miracle of life flowing. Ceremony, sacred ground, open dialogues, and zen gardens are made to help us for this. They help with keeping our priorities straight. What is real is important and primary in life. What we make real can be changed and is secondary in life. The good thing about this is that it's already happening. Our responsibility is mostly about not standing in the way.

The more successful a new paradigm becomes, the more important it is to keep our ego in a secondary position. Serving the master (life), not replacing it.

I have written these steps as a recipe, like sequential steps, so our left hemisphere can understand it. Obviously, this is not a linear, logical, or mechanical thing to do. All four 'steps' are not really steps at all. They happen all at once and need each other to make it work.

You can easily see that reversing them works also, maybe better even. Trust life, create the conditions for healing, remove the causes, understand we are/were the problem. Making it a spiral is also an improvement, it's never finished, or 'done'. Reality is always moving. Where they become realistic is when we start to live from the awareness that everything influences everything all the time. The four steps need each other and will happen at the same time, or not at all. It's the same with the right column of the tables in our chapter entitled "Backwards". Where we also experience them all together. Curing a body are not fixed steps, but principles that guide a process. A process that help us to live from the whole, which is a humble process of getting closer to reality each day. Discovering as many perspectives as possible to what is true.

The final insight for curing our 'spiritual body' is that this is an inclusive process, not excluding anything that is already happening. For our left hemisphere everything is a competition that we should win and something else has to lose. For our right hemisphere it is about competition and cooperation, harmony, balance, belonging, and generosity. A process of non-doing and healing will only work together with a process of changing everything. From technology and legislation to our habits and rituals. We need it all together at the same time. Excluding nothing. Accelerating by including everything. As it is.

Whatever it is you're passionate about and is an expression of your talents, Embodying Reality will increase it. The way you approach it is from the whole, instead of from the parts up. From love, not for love. We still cook based on a recipe we just start to taste in between and adjust accordingly. Presencing reality, as it presents itself to us before we give it labels.

In the new constitution we are going to write as a human species, the first principle should be:

We, the people, take care of what is real and everything we make real we keep in service to what is real.

The path of the black sheep is a brutal and beautiful path. It's a wild path, where we start to Embody Reality. It provides the necessary opposing strength to the power of humans, which it so desperately needs. There is no trust system for being a black sheep. It's about being and healing and other people's stories only distract us from walking this path. So it's good that no platform or group of people claim the path of the black sheep. It would put Iron John back in a cage. Keeping our golden ball hidden in our subconscious.

Thankfully there are more ways to truth that have helped me to fall into reality on a daily basis. Hopefully they will help you too. In no particular order.

Phenomenology, the study of what emerges. It is about learning to see a phenomenon without wanting to label, change or control it.

Etymology, the origin of words. So we can embody our language in a shared rooted meaning.

Therapy, creating space for people so they can lead their lives again.

Philosophy, to learn to ask the right questions and know how things are meant to work. To keep systems of trust grounded in their essence.

Humor, memes, poetry and jokes, because our left hemisphere doesn't understand it. Through them we can share the implicit story of our right hemisphere with others.

History, so we can learn from the past and stop making the same mistakes. Especially, exploiting the whole for a part of it.

Holism and gestalt, to learn to see the whole before the parts.

Ceremony and sacred ground. Doing anything with a beginning, middle and end in the awareness of something greater than our perspective. It usually involves a performance. Where you honor and respect the miracle of life and fall into reality again and again.

Art, where we materialize our ever expanding idea of reality. I also think a global art piece is a good output of the four years of not adding anything. Honoring everything that still is, mourning everything we have lost and respecting the gift of life.

Via negativa. The study of what not to do.

Celebration. The miracle of life is enough reason to start celebrating every moment you feel like it. And if you don't feel like it for a long time it helps to do it anyway. Celebrating and complementing other people achievements in 'letting go' instead of 'fitting in more' is also a powerful tool in helping other people on their path to authenticity.

Embodying Reality means to embody a mystery, non-knowing, non-doing, flowing in a field of energy through death, rebirth, wisdom and what is sacred. It's an invitation to start taking life very seriously and taking our own stories a lot less seriously than before.

If anything, this book is a great example of what not to do. I think I broke every rule I wrote about what sustainability needs. I wrote that the myth is unnameable, only to name it. I wrote that we don't need new stories, only to create a new story. I wrote that you can't encourage others to go on a wild path, just to say that we need more people on a wild path. I wrote that there are no lists to follow in order to do things right, just to proceed to give lists on how to do things right. I wrote that the biggest problem in the world is our idea of how things should be, which again tells others exactly how things should be. Clearly, I have become what I fight against. I comfort myself with the idea that I know I am part of the problem (and therefore at a place of creation). Looking for truth really is a very human path.

Remember, the message of this book is not in the text, but in your reaction to the text. This book is my imagined reality and therefore this is my work. Learning to let go of my own story and learning to see the whole before seeing the parts. I can only see reality within my own shortcomings. Your work is in the white spaces of these pages. What emerged during your reading? What came, or wants to come, into motion? Listen to your river below the river. Follow the signs of your road. That is where your journey into the unknown begins. The best way to deal with our myth is as a secret. Which has now become our secret.

Afterword

The best experience this book has to offer is reading it again somewhere in the near future. You'll find that you read completely new things in it, that it triggers new things in yourself. You'll discover that you didn't quite understand it the first time, the second time, or the third time. The content of this book will continue to unfold and it's never quite finished. The white spaces of these pages truly are a mystery.

The old trees and forests are my gateway to reality. My allies to keep Embodying Reality. Which is as brutal as it is beautiful. If you want to join me, for a ceremony, for sharing, for that feeling of adventure and freedom. You can follow me on: www.embodyingreality.com.

For now, I wish for you as many problems as you can handle. Best of luck.

Bibliography

Charles C. Mann, *The Wizard and the Prophet: Two Remarkable Scientists and Their Dueling Visions to Shape Tomorrow's World*, Random House USA Inc., 2018.

Christine Downing, *The Long Journey Home - Re-Visioning the Myth of Demeter and Persephone for Our Time*, 1994

Clarissa Pinkola Estés, *Women Who Run With the Wolves: Myths and Stories of the Wild Woman Archetype*, Ebury publishing, 1989.

DT Suzuki, *Essays on Zen Buddhism*, Grove Press, 1961.

Daniel Kahneman, *Thinking Fast and Slow*, Penguin Books Ltd, 2012.

David D. Haskell, *The Song of Trees: Stories From Nature's Great Connectors*, Penguin Putnam Inc., 2018.

David Deida, *The way of the superior man*, Plexus, 1997

Iain McGilchrist, *The Matter With Things - The Unmaking of our World*, 2021.

Jaap Voigt, *Dao de Jing van Lao Tzu vertaald door Jaap Voigt*, EF & EF media, 2011.

Jack Zipes, *The Complete First Edition The Original Folk & Fairy Tales of the Brothers Grimm*, Princeton University press, 2014.

James Lovelock, *Gaia: A New Look at Life on Earth*, Oxford University Press.

Jan Geurtz, *Verslaafd aan liefde: de weg naar zelfacceptatie en geluk in relaties*, Ambo, 2009.

Joseph Campbell, *The Hero with a Thousand Faces*, New World Library, 1997.

Liu I-ming, *De innerlijke I Tjing het boek der veranderen als meditatie*, Felix Uitgeverij, 1986.

Merrelyn Emery, *The Search Conference: A Powerful Method for Planning Organizational Change and Community Action,* John Wiley & Sons Inc., 1996.

Nassim Nicholas Taleb, *Antifragile: Things That Gain From Disorder,* Random House, 2012.

Nathaniel Altman, *Sacred Trees,* Gaupo Publishing, 2017.

Pablo Coelho, *The Alchemist,* HarperTorch, 1993.

Ragna Heidweiller, *In voor en tegenspoed, maar alleen als jij de afwas doet,* Nijgh & van Ditmar, 2021.

Robert Bly, *Iron John: A Book About Men,* DA Capo Press, 1990.

Robin Wall Kimmerer, *Braiding Sweetgrass: Indiginous wisdom, scientific knowledge and the Teachings of Plants,* Penguin books ltd, 2020

Susanne Duijvestein - de Boer, *Uitvaart in eigen hand,* de Geus, 2021.

Tachibana Toshitsuna, *Sakuteiki,* mid-to-late 11th century.

Unknown, *Het verhaal aarde: inheemse volken aan het woord voer milieu en ontwikkeling,* Bridges, 1992.

Yuval Noah Harari, *Sapiens: A Brief History of Humankind,* Thomas Rap, 2017.

CPSIA information can be obtained
at www.ICGtesting.com
Printed in the USA
JSHW022125051222
34373JS00005B/27